ISLAM IN EUROPE

"Nilüfer Göle is a leading sociologist who is as familiar with France as she is with Turkey, and therefore with the sensibilities of their respective citizens. In this book, the fruit of many years' reading and observation, she traces the civilizational challenges posed by the contemporary encounter between Muslims and non-Muslims in Europe. A central question that she asks is whether Europe is an identity or a project, and it is clear that she hopes it is first and foremost the latter. Written with rare insight and generosity of spirit, Göle's book offers readers a meditation on one way in which people from very different traditions can live together without animus in an interconnected modern world."

—Talal Asad, CUNY, author of numerous books including *On Suicide Bombing* and *Formations of the Secular: Christianity, Islam, Modernity*

"Nilüfer Göle is a force to be reckoned with. Throughout Europe, she is brilliant on television, at panel discussions, and in academic settings. Professor Göle finds that the urbanization of Islam has brought about fundamental changes in the faith, updating and individualizing it. Islam in Europe is losing its collective hold, which drew on traditional values that developed more than a millennium earlier in the desert. In her view . . . every [terrorist] attack reactivates religious doctrines and redraws the boundaries between Islam as terrorism defines it and the modern world it is condemning."   —*Die Zeit*

"Modernity is . . . shaped, invented by values that were not the values of Muslim countries. That is one of the basic reasons for the separation between the modern world and the Muslim world, this either/or partition. If you are modern, you can't be a Muslim. But now we are going beyond this division—you can be both Muslim and modern."

—Nilüfer Göle, on PBS's *Frontline*

ISLAM IN EUROPE

The Lure of Fundamentalism and the Allure of Cosmopolitanism

NILÜFER GÖLE

Translated by Steven Rendall

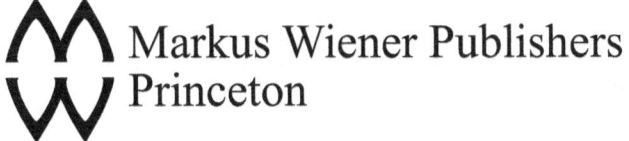
Markus Wiener Publishers
Princeton

Copyright © 2011 by Markus Wiener Publishers for the updated English edition with a new introduction.
Copyright © 2005 by Galaade Éditions for the original French edition entitled *Interpénétrations: L'Islam et l'Europe*.

This work, published as part of the program of aid for publication, received support from the French Ministry of Foreign Affairs and the Cultural Service of the French Embassy in the United States.

Cet ouvrage, publié dans le cadre du programme d'aide à la publication, bénéficie du soutien du Ministère des Affaires Etrangères et du Service Culturel de l'Ambassade de France représenté aux Etats-Unis.

All rights reserved. No part of this book may be reproduced or transmitted in any form or by any means, whether electronic or mechanical—including photocopying or recording—or through any information storage or retrieval system, without permission of the copyright owners.

For information, write to Markus Wiener Publishers
231 Nassau Street, Princeton, NJ 08542
www.markuswiener.com

Library of Congress Cataloging-in-Publication Data

Göle, Nilüfer, 1953-
[Interpénétrations. English]
Islam in Europe : the lure of fundamentalism and the allure of cosmopolitanism / Nilüfer Göle ; translated by Steven Rendall.
  p. cm.
Includes bibliographical references.
ISBN 978-1-55876-525-2 (hardcover : alk. paper)
ISBN 978-1-55876-526-9 (pbk. : alk. paper)
1. Islam—Europe. 2. Muslims—Europe. I. Title.
BP65.E8G6613 2010
297.094—dc22
            2010029761

Markus Wiener Publishers books are printed in the United States of America on acid-free paper and meet the guidelines for permanence and durability of the Committee on Production Guidelines for Book Longevity of the Council on Library Resources.

CONTENTS

Introduction 1

CHAPTER 1: The Other Europe 15

CHAPTER 2: Contemporary Islam 31

CHAPTER 3: The Terrorist Moment 53

CHAPTER 4: The Istanbul Attacks and Islamic Scenography 63

CHAPTER 5: Islam and Globalization: Similarity or Alterity? 77

CHAPTER 6: Modernity, Taxonomies: Global and Local 87

CHAPTER 7: Extra-Modernities 97

CHAPTER 8: Secularism, the Public Space, and Islamic Visibility . . 103

CHAPTER 9: Questions of Women, Questions of Civilization? 111

CHAPTER 10: Publics, Republic, and Denied Citizenship 127

CHAPTER 11: The Veil, the Reversal of the Stigma,
and the Quarrel over Women 139

CHAPTER 12: Identifying Europe: Alterizing Turkey? 149

CHAPTER 13: Giving Up European "Purity" 157

Notes 163

Now we are, so to speak, in a system of "mutual co-penetration." We are moving toward a civilization on the global scale. In which differences will probably appear—at least we must hope they do. But these differences will not be of the same nature, they will be internal, and no longer external.

—Claude Lévi-Strauss, *Le Monde*, 22 February 2005

Introduction

Babel

The globalized world brings people into greater proximity, regardless of their differences in language, religion, ethnic, racial origins, and cultural backgrounds. Migration, travel, and new technologies of communication are making geographic frontiers and cultural boundaries permeable and fuzzy; individuals are entering into close contact with one other, experiencing each other's difference, sometimes against their will, and not always in mutual understanding and peace. We are living in a world in which difference, whether linguistic, religious, racial, or cultural, is not contained within national boundaries or regulated by state power alone, but instead becomes mobile and crosses boundaries. However, entering into close relations with other people and cultures is not always a desired experience; often it produces resentment and a fear of losing one's sense of identity, of feeling safe and "at home." The loss of the comfort provided by distance from other people and cultures engenders new social dynamics concerning the experience of difference, spatial proximity, and cultural confrontation, a transversal process in which close encounters between people lead to mutual changes, borrowings, and "co-penetrations"; a process in which resentment and fear, cultural translation or the lack thereof, conflict, and confrontation are involved.

In his movie *Babel*,[1] Alejandro Gonzáles Iñárritu, a Mexican-American film director, depicts with force and originality the perilous dynamics of a global world that brings individuals from very different horizons into closer physical contact. He creates a new genre by telling simultaneously developing, distinct stories in different languages—

English, Spanish, Arabic, Berber, Japanese, and sign language. These stories are juxtaposed, connected, and interdependent, rather than producing one sequential and progressive narrative. They take place in a transversal and transnational world that is not free from miscommunication, fear, and violence. Human beings divided by language, dislocated in space, and unable to communicate with each other find themselves interconnected in a series of unprecedented dramatic events. In spite of their differences in language, class, and civilization, each of them finds that his or her fate is determined by the others and converges with theirs.

The movie travels from remote villages in the mountains of Morocco to the closely monitored desert border between the United States and Mexico, passing through flourishing urban Tokyo, the center of modern angst, before arriving in Morocco. The travelers, a privileged American couple, experience helplessness and vulnerability when the wife is accidentally shot in the neck and has to rely on the kindness and medical care of Moroccan villagers. The bullet was shot from a gun meant to keep the jackals away from a herd but which has become a toy for the underaged shepherds. It was given to the children's father by a Japanese man passing through the village on a hunting trip. Meanwhile, without the consent of their parents, the overprotected children of the American family travel to Mexico with the family's housekeeper, whose son is getting married. They all enjoy a festive and joyful party. However, recrossing the border to go home becomes a terrifying experience for both the children and their Mexican nanny; suspected of being clandestine migrants and pursued by the police, they get lost in the desert.

In each of these separate stories, we witness a constant tension, incongruity, and mistranslation between the intentions of the characters, the unexpected and dramatic consequences of their behavior, and the meanings given to their acts. In the background, the voice-over of the media broadcasts the discursive power of the Western world, commenting, (mis)interpreting the chain of events, and using the vocabulary of terrorism, clandestine migrants, and kidnapping. The police in Morocco, in Tokyo, and at the Mexican border illustrate the ways local events are captured in international dynamics that give way to a politics of suspicion and forms of governmentality ranging from brute power (villagers beaten to death, children shot by police) to new technologies of power (DNA tests, the professionalization of mediators and interpreters) and policing. We discover the ways in which the distinct stories of border crossing—a tourist couple, a migrant worker, and a hunter who have little in common—chance to meet and become interconnected and interdependent in spite of their social differences and lack of cultural and linguistic communication. Yet they all share emotions of loss, fear, pain, anguish, and tears, and none of these emotions will be lost in translation.[2]

The myth of Babel, from which the movie borrows its name, tells the story of humans who attempt to build a tower that would reach the heavens but thereby incur God's wrath and are punished by being scattered over the face of the earth in a state of confusion and lack of communication. The movie depicts the world in which we live from this perspective of displacement, confusion, fear, and anxiety. The myth of Babel is a lesson on the consequences of arrogance and unchecked ambition. Similarly, the movie shows how modern Westerners' claim to be autonomous and independent from the "rest" of the world is an illusion. Once the comfort of distance and protection maintained by geographical borders and cultural boundaries disappear, people see that they are vulnerable and dependent on the others.

The film also resonates with the ways in which American citizens, during the 9/11 attacks against the World Trade Center, encountered the "third-world" Taliban movement on their own soil, discovered their vulnerability, and experienced in the middle of New York City the turmoil and destruction one might expect to face in the streets of Kabul. The Twin Towers, which contained individuals representing cultures, religions, and languages from all over the world, became a metaphor of the contemporary myth of the Tower of Babel. The World Trade Center was built with great engineering skill and an industrial arrogance that defied space, and it was destroyed by a religious arrogance that despised the value of human lives, commitment to the affairs of this world, and the daily routines of work.

A remapping of the world is underway; the hierarchies of different parts of the world—the supremacy of the first world, and the dependence of the third world—are unsettled. New centers are emerging, such as Tokyo in the film, but so is the experience of hypermodernity, however introverted and mute (as in the case of the deaf young girl). In this new world, new fault lines emerge, as represented by Morocco and Mexico, two countries that border on the West. Muslims and Mexicans, two immigrant groups, are seen in the film as a threat—sometimes regardless of their intentions—to the security of members of the American family (the couple being imperiled by terrorism and the children by kidnapping). The porousness of borders and boundaries risks shattering the privileges of modern Western citizens hermetically sealed off from unwanted customs, cultural differences, and uncivilized behavior, living in secure gated communities and in nations with boundaries under surveillance.

The idea that the tranquility of Western civilization is threatened is not merely a fiction but a widely shared opinion in real-life politics. Samuel P. Huntington's influential thesis of a "clash of civilizations" is based upon the observation that Western civilization, although it remains the most powerful, is declining into a multi-civilizational system. According to him, in "the new world the most pervasive, dangerous and important conflicts will not be between social classes, rich and poor or other economically defined groups but between peoples belonging to different cultural entities."[3] Countries that do not belong to one of these entities are "torn countries" experiencing the civilizational clash within themselves. Among such countries, Huntington singles out Mexico and Turkey. In his view, both these countries seek to incorporate Western values and adhere to Western civilization, but such a civilizational shift is almost impossible to achieve, since it requires that three conditions be met simultaneously—the elite has to be enthusiastic about this move, the public has to be willing to acquiesce in the redefinition of its identity, and last but not least the host civilization, namely the West, has to be willing to embrace the converts.[4]

Indeed, the debates surrounding Turkey's candidacy for admission to the European Union (EU) and the presence of Muslim immigrants have brought to the fore the resentment and fear European citizens feel regarding Turkey's inclusion in Europe. The Turkish presence is perceived as a potential threat to the "civilizational" unity of Europe. The fact that Turkey is the only country with a Muslim majority that is a candidate for the EU, and also a country from which Muslims emigrate to Europe, crystallized in different ways the presence of Muslims both inside and outside Europe. Turkish membership is feared as a "Trojan horse" that would bring Islam into Christian lands; its admission is perceived as a "forced marriage" imposed by political elites but resented by European peoples. It would mean changing the historical memory of Europe and de-emphasizing its victory over the Ottoman Empire at the gates of Vienna in 1683. In sum, Turkish membership in the EU has become a matter of identity for Europeans (rather than for Turks, as was expected), who have expressed their unwillingness to "blur" European identity and include other Eastern, noncolonized Muslim countries, along with the legacy of the Ottoman Empire.

Drawing on the examples of Mexico and Turkey, we can argue that both countries, although in different ways, have come to be "border countries" with the West (Mexico with the United States, Turkey with the European Union); they mark the West's geographical and cultural boundaries. Like Turks in Europe, the Mexican immigrants to the United States, in the eyes of those who are keen to defend their boundaries and national identity, create a potential threat to the cultural "core values" and political integrity of the United States, because they are considered incapable of speaking the American language, claiming civil rights, and acquiring virtues common to all Americans.[5]

Looking into the mirror held up by the Hispanic and Muslim presence, the "two distinct Wests"—America and Europe—find themselves asking who they are and asserting common, "core" values. In that sense Muslims and Mexicans become the "constitutive outside" for debating national identities and values, and therefore have an impact on the redefinitions of Europe and North America's self-concept and self-presentation. Jacques Derrida's notion of the constitutive outside is a reminder of the irreducibility of difference ("*l'irréductibilité de l'alterité*") that makes closure impossible and opens up the possibility of new ways of relating self to Other.[6] Uncertainty and the possibility of the emergence of difference and disagreement are bound together as the very condition of democratic society. The power of democracy, as Claude Lefort argues, is the production of "dissensus" and its capacity to receive and preserve "indetermination."[7] From this perspective, the entry of Islam into European debates can be seen as playing the role of the constitutive outside that instigates a debate on difference and opens up the established boundaries of consensus.

Islam—thought to be a ghostly presence from the past, a relic expected to fade away with the process of modernization and secularization—is now entering the contemporary European public sphere. As a result of immigration and globalization, the issues regarding Islam are not confined to one geographic space, such as the Middle East, or to a Muslim-majority nation-state such as Turkey or Iran, but have become part of European reality. The presumed time lag between those who are advanced and those who are not is disappearing. The geographical separation between those who are considered to be civilized and the rest ceases to reassure. Europeans and Muslims have now become coevals and share—not always willingly or equally—the same cities, schools, leisure activities, political parties, and daily life.

This is the story I am attempting to tell in this book; today, Islam and Europe are becoming interconnected (although not for the first time in history) in unprecedented ways; Muslims are facing new questions arising from their life experiences in Europe as members of a minority religion living in a secular and pluralistic setting, while Europe is revisiting its own identity and values in the mirror of Muslim presence and difference. I propose to frame this process in terms of an "interpenetration" of Islam and Europe and to highlight its embodied, gendered, and violent dimensions.

In ways similar to the movie *Babel* and to the work of the Turkish-German filmmaker Fatih Akin (whom I discuss in the next chapter), I will follow several narratives developing simultaneously, seemingly in isolation from each other, in which Muslim migrants and indigenous Europeans become interconnected in unexpected ways and against their will and their way of seeing things. While the presence of Muslims in Europe is not a recent phenomenon, and Europeans have long had a relationship with the Islamic world, the way Europeans and Muslims have become aware of each other's presence, confronting their differences and debating the aesthetic and ethical dimensions of modernity, presents a contemporary challenge. We need to tease out the dynamics of cultural confrontation in spatial proximity—a process that brings to our attention a series of issues in relation to Islamic visibility that were not previously on the public agenda of European democracies.

The mute symbols of Islam
and the appearance of Muslims in Europe

Two main symbols of the Islamic presence in Europe have recently provoked debate. Despite the differences between national contexts, histories of migration, and changing notions of secularism, practices of Islamic covering for women—following different manifestations and semantic shifts, namely, from headscarf, veiling, hijab, nikap, to burka—and the demands for the construction of mosques have captured the greatest public attention.

One wonders when and how a symbol or an object that is not visible because it is insignificant or so familiar as to have become imperceptible suddenly becomes "visible"—indeed, ostentatious and disturbing in the eyes of a public. I could not have imagined that one day mosques would achieve a disturbing visibility, minarets and mosques would be separated, and the mosque as a tranquil space of prayer and friendly sociability would be feared.

It might be unexpected that in a country with a Muslim majority like Turkey, the historical and cultural symbols of Islam might also cease to be parts of the field of a familiar, peaceful, and immutable heritage, and begin to develop a new visibility in the public field, and awakening religious and political divisions.

Without its slender minarets, Istanbul would lose a part of its soul. Minarets, in the eyes of the inhabitants—pious and secular, Muslim and non-Muslim—are part of the familiar landscape, of the common heritage. Crossing the Galata Bridge I never tire of contemplating with wonder the panorama of Istanbul in which emerge, like drawings, the silhouettes of its tall, slim minarets. Today many rightly regret that the new mosques built in contemporary Turkey are far from equaling those of the great architect Mimar Sinan (d. 1588 CE), who worked during the glorious days of the Ottoman Empire and to whom we owe the Istanbul landscape. Contemporary mosques, for the most part, lack architectural innovation, refinement, and proportion between the dome and the minarets. Likewise, the calls to prayer, since the adoption of cassettes and loudspeakers, have become a source of ongoing public debate over whether they constitute a nuisance, a kind of noise pollution. But public debate is not confined to these subjects. The projects of reopening Hagia Sophia as a place of prayer for Muslims and of constructing a new mosque at Taksim Square in the heart of Istanbul have given rise in the past two decades to a lively and passionate controversy—a controversy that divides citizens who position themselves against signs of Islamization and those who would like to mark the social rise of Islam by putting a religious imprint on Turkey's public spaces. The split between the religious culture and those who declare themselves defenders of secularism runs through the current public life of Turkey. A poem fueled the polemic when Tayyip Erdoğan recited it in a speech given in the province of Siirt in 1997[8]: "the mosques are our barracks, the domes our helmets, the minarets our bayonets and the faithful our soldiers."[9]

Pious Muslims and mosques with their domes and minarets ceased to be part of a peaceful landscape and became images of war in the form of barracks, helmets, bayonets, and soldiers. The verses were written in the context of the war for national independence and were attributed to one of the well-known nationalist poets. However, Erdoğan, who later became the prime minister of Turkey in 2003, was sentenced and jailed for "incitement to religious hatred" for having recited these verses. European debates replicate in surprising ways the Turkish ones, and, as we will see, the same poem has been reproduced in anti-mosque campaigns and posters printed all over Europe.

The passage of Islam into Europe acquires distinctive traits and confronts Muslims with a series of novel questions. In Europe, minarets and mosques face "existential" problems; the minarets are mute without the muezzins' call to prayer, and the mosques are discreet. However, some European democracies, with a view to both security and openness, are seeking to increase the visibility of places of worship, inviting them to come out of their cellars and garages into the daylight. Nevertheless, the significance of allowing the mosque its visibility is not self-evident; which forms, which spaces, and which concepts can it be accorded? Does a mosque always have a dome and a minaret? Can we have a mosque that would not be identifiable as such? Can we separate, as the Swiss would like to do, the minarets from the mosques? How can we invent new architectural forms in response to the landscape and the heritage of their surroundings? Can we replace the word *mosque*, a word that some fear, with *place of prayer*? How can the mosque combine different ethnic communities? For example, do Arabs pray in the Pakistani mosques in Birmingham? Do North Africans and other Muslim minorities pray in Turkish mosques in Berlin? By which criteria should one decide the language of the sermon? How might one rethink the space of the mosque for women, for youth, and as the site of diverse activities? Could women pray alongside men? Should women have separate places in mosques? Muslim women challenge traditional habits and unwritten laws and request better accommodation and treatment in mosques. Recently, Muslim women protested separation by praying in the main hall at the Islamic Center in Washington D.C., running the risk of getting arrested.[10] Muslim women "making their case with a pray-in" ask for a decent, clean, quiet space to pray and ask to be consulted when mosques are designed.[11] The recently constructed "Şakirin" mosque in Istanbul (2009) is considered the first to be designed by a female interior designer and in a way that welcomes women.

Islamic prayer raises a wide range of issues: the hours for prayer and the places where it occurs, the connections between cultural institutions and mosques, religious markers in the landscape, architectural forms, the home-grown education of imams, local ethnic lineages, global financial links, gender segregation, and privacy.

The mosque provides an interface between the urban environment, Muslim citizens, religious pluralism, and governance. Accepting its visibility leads to a series of negotiations and regulations—aesthetic, religious, financial, architectural, and spatial—and therefore encourages an engagement by all sides in the process of making it an object of a common heritage in progress. The Swiss referendum (by popular initiative), which enacted, by a majority vote, the ban on constructing minarets (November 29, 2010), has imposed what could not be negotiated. It might be democratic in the procedural sense, but since the vote imposes the nonnegotiable and thereby slows the process of engagement and negotiation, it has an undemocratic significance. It does not open up the possibility of transforming the relation of self with the Other, but instead, by establishing the national boundaries and consensus, excludes it. The minaret referendum bears witness to the difficulty Swiss society has in recognizing the presence of newly settled Muslims and in making a place for them in public life. People's feeling that

Islam is invading their territory, the fear of losing their "home," has fed these debates. In speeches, Muslims have been asked to build their minarets "back home"; posters depict them as threatening "strangers" and thus symbolically expel them. All the semantics of the debate lead us to think that the recognition of Islam and of Muslims as citizens poses problems within Swiss society in particular but also in other European contexts. What is conveyed is the desire to block the transition from immigrant status to citizenship rights by refusing to acknowledge equal rights to participate in public life.

The leitmotif of the debate, protecting oneself and one's home from this invading religion, conceals as well a reluctance to give up Swiss-born citizens' monopoly on their public space. The undemocratic character of this vote resides in its expression of a desire to contain and determine public space in strict equivalence with an essentialist conception of the nation, without opening it to the plurality of its citizens. In another respect, Muslims, with their multiple attachments—to languages, ethnic groups, religion, and the *ummah*—disrupt the national definition of citizenship and arouse suspicions regarding their loyalty. The definition of a public space identified with a preestablished national community can only create tensions and exclusions in a world traversed by migratory and transnational dynamics, whether they are religious, economic, or cultural.

The referendum, far from remaining confined to the Swiss context, has resonated in other national contexts and has rendered a transnational, European aspect to the debate. Some deplore the Swiss ban as an error not to be repeated; others have applauded the courage to say out loud what everybody thinks in private. Polls conducted in France have revealed a favorable opinion of the limitation on the construction of mosques. The Swiss poster widely used in the anti-minaret campaign has been reproduced in many different national contexts. It shows the national flag pierced by minarets portrayed as missiles and a female silhouette totally covered in a black fabric, appearing as faceless and obscured. The poster conveys the feeling of being invaded and threatened by Islam, reproducing the symbols of Islamic visibility (minarets and burkas) as weapons threatening values of national security and gender equality. Minarets are separated from mosques and represented as weapons, and have thus lost their pious and innocent significance, that is, calling for prayers; similarly, in the poster, women are dehumanized and faceless and represent obscurantism. Such a politics of representation turns enmity into stigmatization and symbolic violence. The same anti-minaret poster has been reproduced by analogous populist parties in other countries, the Swiss flag being replaced by that of Britain, France, Germany, Belgium, or Italy; hence, the visual suggestion that the minarets are invading national territories and women in burkas are threatening cultural values is reproduced and has entered into circulation. In the English versions, the verses recited by Tayyip Erdoğan are included. In public debates throughout Europe, these same verses have been constantly reproduced. We see how the debate about the minarets in particular and the visibility of Islam in general generates transnational dynamics and assemblages of disparate elements. We see that even England and Switzerland—one insular, the other not even a member of the EU—enter the European public field. Islam makes its opponents audible and visible, and countries that are minor or peripheral move to the center of the European public agenda (as in the case of the cartoon controversy in Denmark). A remapping of European publics and politics is underway; right-wing populist parties from across Europe met in Germany to follow in Switzerland's footsteps and to look into the possibility of an EU-wide minaret ban.[12]

Fear of Islam is instrumentalized by various populist parties, and proponents of "anti-Islamization policies" are looking for ways to gain popularity and resonance within the silent majority. Marginal political figures such as Oscar Freysinger in Switzerland, Geert Wilders in the Netherlands, and Philippe de Villiers in France, have contributed to the transformation of national political agendas across Europe and have won notoriety in their fight against the Islamic presence in Europe.

Likewise, eliciting the visceral and emotional by appealing to irrational fears (phobias) and personal feelings risks creating a public space plagued by prejudices. It is largely around the theme of Islamic visibility that collective passions and public debates are mobilized today. These questions put the public space to the test of a democratic debate that can be inflamed by promoting such a politics of fear. European democracies have developed by making a distinction between opinion and truth, by advocating the use of reason in public debate. The current political populism threatens this European tradition of the "enlightened public." The public sphere is in danger of losing its role as the ideal expression of democracy and of common sense, and of becoming the site of sacralization of public opinion and of contagion of the sensational and scandalous.

The headscarf at school, the burka on the street, the mosque in the city, and the minarets in the landscape indicate the presence of Muslim actors in daily life (sometimes with an exacerbated religiosity that praises withdrawal from social life), but they also place on the public agenda the debate regarding the secular norms of common space.

The public visibility of these religious and cultural signs of Islam expresses the presence of Muslim actors in European countries. The minarets and mosques reveal the pious Muslim actor in public life just as the veil, another mute symbol, reveals the female Muslim actor. This visibility attests to Muslims' desire to stay in European society, their claim to freedom of conscience, and their right to worship and dress according to their personal interpretation of their religion. Paradoxically, Islam has become a political and cultural way for immigrants to pursue their quest for recognition, and thus it indicates in turn their particular citizenship in the public space of Europe. This new visibility marks the end of a stage in migration and in integration, lived experience, and modes of appropriation of public space in Europe. What lies behind the controversies surrounding Islam is the difficulty of recognizing this passage from the foreigner (immigrant) to the citizen.

* * *

This book is a product of a convergence between my personal trajectory and a given moment in the history of Europe during which debates about the presence of Islam in general and about Turkish membership in the European Union in particular have been of the utmost importance. When I moved from Istanbul to Paris in 2001, I did not expect "Europe" to become my main focus of research and intellectual interest, nor did I expect Europe to begin a period of rapid change and become part of the intellectual and historical intrigue between Islam and modernity. I did not deliberately choose to study Europe, Europe imposed itself on me. I moved to France, but I had the feeling that France also came closer to me by debating issues related to Islam and Turkey.

Over the past two decades, themes that had previously been considered outside European boundaries, confined to "Muslim" countries, to the "Middle East," began to affect Europe and its politics. Muslim girls' insistence on adopting Islamic head covering in French public schools triggered a more general debate about secularism and feminism. To me, coming from Turkey where these issues have been debated since the early 1980s, the French debate seemed like déjà vu. When one moves toward the West, one has the awkward habit of thinking that one is entering modern times and the land of innovation. However, I found myself in the midst of a debate with which I was already familiar in Turkey, as if history had been reversed and was running counter-clockwise.

The debates on the Islamic headscarf and the Turkish candidacy for membership in the EU implicated me personally as well, in all kinds of places, ranging from dinner tables with friends and meetings with colleagues to more public and media-oriented discussions. I often had the impression that it was difficult to escape some sort of identification with my national or religious affiliation. Independent of my own will, in the eyes of the others, I was supposed to wear either the "fez" (although the fez, as a sign of the Ottoman Empire, was abolished with the modern republic, it is still used to depict and caricature Turkish difference in Europe) or the "headscarf." I was asked to take a position "for" or "against" on various issues. Given the tone of certainty and rejection in these debates, being identifiable as Turkish and Muslim may not have been psychologically rewarding or pleasing to others, but for me it was certainly a privileged position (location) in which I witnessed personally the emotional substrate that fueled fear and resentment in relation to Islam and the seismic, oppositional forces at work in the making of European history. The accidental trajectory of my personal life was starting to have a particular resonance with European history in this novel phase of the encounter between Turkey, Islam, and Europe. My individual biography and European history converged at a given location and time. I found my personal trajectory to be connected more than ever to people living in Europe, whether they were Muslims or not.

To link biography to history requires a particular quality of mind that C. Wright Mills called the "sociological imagination" (1959). It is the quality of mind that enables us to understand what is going on in the world and what is happening within ourselves. It enables its possessor to understand the larger historical scene in terms of its meaning for her inner life. As Mills reminds us, "in many ways it is a terrible lesson; in many ways a magnificent one." *Islam in Europe* is the product of this dual point of view. It is my hope that it will help open up a new mental space between the two, at the interstices, in mutual borrowings and inter-breeding. This is a book that tries to enhance our awareness of the interconnectedness of our individual and collective histories, no matter what our intentions and desires may be.

CHAPTER 1

The Other Europe

The wall and the bridge

How can we live together? Every society repeatedly asks the age-old question about what unites us: religion, memory, the state, common interests, the collective consciousness. It is a question that has become particularly captivating for today's Europeans, for two reasons. First, the existence of the project and the very idea of the European Union signify the necessity of finding a new way of rethinking the social bond among Europeans, beyond the framework of nation-states. Second, the presence of Islam in Europe introduces a new dimension, a cultural, religious, and civilizational difference that challenges the established ways European nations live together. Islam erupts in the social debates that are the most constitutive of contemporary European consciousness: debates about secular values in the definition of the individual, the equality of the sexes, feminism and homosexuality, freedom of expression in the artistic and literary domain, and also the relationship to history and the transmission of the collective memory through education. The confrontations between secular feminism and the Islamic veil, art and blasphemy, the memory of the Holocaust and the colonial past, have thrown the debate about the common values of Europe into turmoil. With Islam, the categories of sexuality, art, and memory are found at the heart of public politics. As Islam, the "forgotten" of history, increases in importance, the direction and the tone of the debate on Europe's common values are changing.

Islam constitutes a challenge to our ways of conceiving of the secular modernity of Europe, a challenge that we prefer to ignore by reducing it to the questions of immigration, economics, or security. Today, Islam is the place where the question of "how to live together" is raised in a double process: that of expansion and the inclusion of the countries of Eastern Europe and that of the cultural confrontation with the "Islamic difference." The end of communism and Muslim immigration constitute the two processes through which Europe is renewing itself and changing in nature. However, there is no symmetrical relationship between these two processes. While one is located in a relation of inclusion, the other is defined as the Other of Europe. The history of the candidacies of Poland (the most religious of the Christian countries) and of Turkey (the most secular of the Muslim countries) for admission to the European Union illustrates this contrast. Poland, a country in which Catholic religious values are influential (including at the legal level, where abortion is still prohibited), is being included in the European Union in a process that is fairly natural and smooth (which prompts Poles to say that for the first time in history they are receiving without giving). On the other hand, Turkey, a much older member of the "European club," has to cope with a debate in which the very legitimacy of its candidacy is put into question. The fall of the Berlin wall, by putting an end to communist alterity, has changed the situation in a way that favors European expansion toward the east. On the other hand, the debate on European identity continues, marked by this anxiety with regard to the Other, to Islamic alterity.

The reference, as in the case of the Turkish candidacy, to the geographical, cultural, and religious values of Europe in order to distinguish the current members of the European Union from Islam and protect against it, raises the question whether a new "wall" is being built in Europe. The fall of the Berlin wall has become a "realm of memory" for constructing a new Europe that conceives itself through expansion and the inclusion of the ex-communist countries. Why doesn't the destruction of the bridge at Mostar represent such a symbol for Europeans? The extermination of the Muslims of Bosnia is recorded but not recognized as genocide. However, the future of European politics depends on the way it includes the Muslims of Europe, just as it includes the citizens of the ex-communist countries.

Europe is constructed as much by the commemoration of its past as by what it forgets, by a selective memory that recalls some things and excludes others. For many Europeans—citizens, intellectuals, politicians—the fall of the Berlin wall may seem constitutive of their history, of their collective identity, contrary to the bridge at Mostar, which is recognized for its architectural beauty and its ability to connect peoples, religions, and communities at the heart of Europe. How can we envisage "living together" without referring to these places where people meet, mix, and inter-breed? We can wonder about the absence of the metaphor of the bridge in the construction of Europe, the rhetoric of borders that gives priority to the limits that separate, divide, and protect, like a wall, instead of seeing these borders as a point of passage that makes it possible to exchange, to trade, to go from one side to the other.

How will Europe conceive of itself, as a protective wall or as a place of mixing and exchange? The answer is not easy and draws on both registers. The more Europe becomes a place of cultural heterogeneity, the more Europeans express their fear of losing their "purity," of seeing their heritage erased, of feeling threatened by the presence and the difference of immigrants. For their part, the immigrants feel disappointed, frustrated at not being recognized as Europeans, of always being reduced to their national, religious, or ethnic origins, of being experienced as the Other of Europe. The fabric connecting "immigrants" and "natives" in Europe is not easily woven; distrust, fear, and mutual rejection often constitute the affective bedrock of an impossible relationship. The two groups are in proximity to each other, they share the same soil, the same spaces, cities, schools, work, markets. And yet they do not meet each other, or, more precisely, they do not know that they meet, that their history is henceforth linked, more by constraint than by a mutual desire for peace.

But we cannot understand developing Europe without speaking of the Other Europe. The goal of this book is to show that the Other Europe is not external and passive but participates in the process of European change, in the way in which Europe shapes and conceives of itself.

New images of Europe

At a conference in Berlin (November 18, 2006) attended by many intellectuals and politicians, the filmmaker Wim Wenders said in substance that the soul of Europe was old and that in order to survive and inspire dreams, it needed to recognize itself in new images that take cultural diversity into account.

In his films, Fatih Akin offers new images, a new European way of seeing that allows us to conceive differently the question of diversity. Akin, who was born to Turkish immigrants in Germany and grew up and still lives there, inquires into the presence/absence of connections between Turks and Germans. Here, I will take the theme of "failed" encounters as a leitmotif of his film *Auf der anderen Seite* (*The Edge of Heaven*, 2007). The first generation of Turkish immigrants did not know the German language or the cultural codes of communication and behavior in Germany. They probably felt safer, affectively speaking, keeping to themselves. On the other hand, the new generation found itself in a nonplace, with the loss of the comfort of being among other Turks, no longer seeing themselves as part of the Turkish "community" on the one hand and engaged in an encounter and an exchange with Germans that proved to be difficult. For Akin, who is part of this second generation, the absence of an encounter between Turks and Germans has become a source of questions and even of suffering.

Fatih Akin shows that through these "failed" encounters between Turks and Germans, personal histories accidentally cross and interconnect to the point of being transformed by these encounters, and this often involves violence and death, without anyone wanting this to happen, without anyone realizing it. He draws a rich gallery of portraits of the two generations, Turks and Germans, choreographing their intersections, their failed encounters, the noncoincidence of their lives that are nonetheless interdependent. Nejat, a young professor of German literature who is of Turkish origin, refined and cultivated, is the son of Ali, the prototype of the first-generation immigrant, violent and affectionate at the same time, who accidentally kills, out of jealousy, a Turkish prostitute from Hamburg named Yeter; she is the mother of the young Kurdish woman activist Ayten, who is to become the mistress of Lotte, the daughter of Susanne (played by Hanna Schygulla, who embodies German counterculture both in her role as a hippie mother and as Fassbinder's favorite actress), who will become acquainted with Nejat in tragic circumstances. Fatih Akin escapes the rigidity of identity-related and national frameworks to enter into the transversality of human relationships, into the circularity of movements, into the constant back-and-forth between the two countries (which also involves coffins). The permanence of the places, of "home," of the return, of the country, is replaced by the movement across borders and zones of encounters.

Fatih Akin does not make films about immigration but about the Other Europe, providing a new view of Europeanness that is worked out in a process of interpenetration and fermentation. His way of seeing, at the intersection of two cultures, fractures the hierarchical relationship between those who are at the center of Europe and those who are at a distance, on the periphery. Speaking of his own generation, he says, "We no longer tell ourselves stories about the margins but rather about the center of society" (*Der Spiegel*, September 28, 2007). He moves the Other, the immigrant, the Turk, to the center, that is, he makes him encounter the German and European imagination. Filmmaking is also working on oneself, on one's own imagination. In his case, we cannot speak of a hybrid identity that is ready-made and already constituted by the hyphen between the Turkish and German identities. Immigration means the loss of a sense of identity and permanent membership in a group. Through his films, Akin works like an archeologist to discover the buried and fragmented Turk within himself. Unlike the films of immigrants in search of work that recount their departure from their villages toward European cities, here the journey takes place in the opposite direction. It is Turkey that attracts him, that fascinates him by being at once familiar and distant, similar and yet different. As he says in the same interview, "In Turkey, I see everything with different eyes," unlike in Hamburg, where everything is familiar to him. He reconstitutes a cultural memory and reconstitutes himself, both as hybrid subject. In the three films (*Head-On, Crossing the Bridge: The Sound of Istanbul,* and *The Edge of Heaven*) where the archeological work is carried out, he tries to reduce to sensorial and visual consciousness everything that survives and resists acculturation, such as ways of cooking, musical rhythms, expressions that are affectionate or not. But these films also make Turks familiar with their own culture by introducing an element of foreignness, "of disturbing foreignness" that some will prefer to reject on the pretext of "orientalism."

They will refuse to recognize themselves in his immigrant, German, European way of seeing. However, Fatih Akin wants to cross bridges without burning them.. These films have no end, no place of arrival or return, no goal of reconnecting. He does not want to make choices about identity or permanent membership in a group. He does not play one off against the other but rather plays both at once, he is in the interstice, the in-between—a position that has the value of a vision, of an alternative space for Another Europe.

Fatih Akin's films allow me to pursue my work on the necessity of opening up the categories of social science that can easily imprison us in an approach based on terms of identity and homogeneous and fixed spaces. The characters in his films, unlike most, are looking for places and not identities. The feeling accompanying the loss of a home does not lead them to shut themselves up in an aesthetics of nostalgia, but rather to make a spatial transgression. This feeling of loss, although it is not symmetrical between the natives and the immigrants, is shared by both. The immigrants have left their original home and seek to become familiar with new places, which implies a transformation and even a subversion of these places. The Europeans, for their part, feel threatened by this intrusion, which is sometimes peasant and sometimes religious, but always kitsch and not in conformity with European civility. They live within the constraint of being in proximity to the Other, of being neighbors, of sharing the same spaces, the soil, the cities, the public parks, apartment buildings, workplaces, schools, parliament, hospitals. Many of them express this feeling as loss, of no longer feeling "at home" but rather being invaded by the number and the difference of Muslim immigrants. Although the same spaces are shared, the habits, the cultural ways of living in them, are not shared.

How can we conceive of cultural diversity in a single space? This is far from being a new question for the social sciences, taken up and debated in the framework of multiculturalism and in relation to the German notion of the public sphere (*Öffentlichkeit*). But these debates presuppose, on the one hand, diversity as a given identity and, on the other hand, a homogeneous notion of the public sphere connected with a national culture. The cinema makes it possible to introduce a more perceptible and more heterogeneous dimension of space. In Akin's films, places are hybrid, a sort of juxtaposition of different cultural habitations. The old Turk, the immigrant father, cultivates his tomato garden in his home in Hamburg, while his son becomes the owner of a German bookstore in Istanbul. One of them feels at home, surrounded by his tomatoes; the other does too, surrounded by these books in German. The places are invested, occupied, inhabited, and thus permanently transformed by the presence of the Other. Does the director have a very nomadic view of places, resembling immigration and Anatolian history? His characters are in movement, traveling, investing in new places in search of traces left by their loved ones who have left, disappeared, been killed; like this German mother from the counter-culture generation who set out in search of her murdered daughter, and who takes up residence in the Bohemian neighborhood of Istanbul.

Death, love, and evil form a universal trilogy that the director works within his films in order to understand human relationships. Far from simplifying or embellishing the history of relations between Turks and Germans, he shows all its complexity and the absence of symmetrical relationships. Although violence proceeds mainly from the Other, the immigrant, the Turk, the latter is a source of attraction, chaotic energy, and fascination. Akin shows us the interweaving of violence and love. He makes love emerge where we would least expect it, between two girls who do not speak the same language and between generations of different national cultures. Reconciliation and forgiveness among generations and cultures (between the German mother and the Turkish son) thus appear as an opportunity to create new connections, to lay the affective foundations for living together.

Akin elaborates a new view of Europe by giving priority to the metaphor of the bridge. By rejecting the permanence of identities, borders that separate, he follows these life trajectories that implicitly interconnect, the way in which each side crosses the bridge (*Crossing the Bridge* is the title of one of his films), which is simultaneously a place and a metaphor that allows individuals to meet and to be transformed by their encounter.

Akin is known for his ability to breathe new life into German cinema by introducing the themes of the foreigner, the Turk, the immigrant. It is said that he pays homage to Rainer Werner Fassbinder. His films also bear the stamp of the psychodramatic style of Turkish cinema. However that may be, he is helping to elaborate European culture by focusing on its margins. The parallel with the Spanish filmmaker Pedro Almodovar seems pertinent regarding progress on the question of cultural difference and Europe. Almodovar's films have shaped the European imagination through their way of appropriating the effects of the European counterculture and the sexual revolution. He films the most unlikely stories about homosexuality, stories that seem, paradoxically, to be our own. His films have never been labeled as marginal or addressed solely to a homosexual audience. In the same way, but in a very different style (more melodramatic than grotesque), Fatih Akin tells Turkish stories that also become German and European stories. The two filmmakers include difference in the whole of social representation and help elaborate a new European imagination.

Like Almodovar, Akin draws on a certain cultural marginality, which he shows both in Berlin and in Istanbul. These "underground" life-spaces are echoed (especially in his film *Head-On*") by a very specific imagination linking two cities, two countries, two cultures, and this is very difficult to imagine between Algiers and Paris, for instance. He also casts a critical eye on religious conservatism. Islam, although it is not central in his films, is identified as a source of the oppression of women by patriarchal power (which exercises moral control over girls' sexuality) or through communal power (which threatens the Turkish prostitute). Although these images describe a certain everyday reality of religious conservatism, they are also stereotypical. These critical representations of Islam and their proximity to a sensitivity to European counter-culture, certainly ease the reception of Akin's films in the European imagination.

Without burning the bridges?

If I mention Fatih Akin's films in this book , that is because I believe that his images can broaden our mental horizon and prevent it from being exclusively critical, imprisoned in opinions, discursive practices, and pre-established, abstract debates. Art opens the way to a more visual, more sensual, more imaginative thought. Akin's films also very strongly echo the approach and the themes of this book. Giving priority to an approach in terms of the interdependency and interconnection of the life stories of Turks and Germans emphasizes a transversal representation of relationships. Leaving behind the logic of immigration, the description of failures to integrate and strategies of adaptation, we are here operating on the same basis in interpreting Europe and its margins. My goal is to provide an interpretation using a double mirror: to read the practices of immigrants and Muslims in the mirror of their European experience and to read the transformations of Europeans' identity in their encounter with the Other, the immigrant and the Muslim.

To understand contemporary Islam, we have to move beyond fixed identity categories. Religion as such is not part of the immigrants' baggage. The process of immigration is accompanied by a certain acculturation in the transmission of religious knowledge, a loss of bearings with respect to authority, to organized religion. Young Muslims who turn to Islam often break with traditional and familial interpretations of religious practice, and seek to study religion in a "scholarly" way by going "to the sources," as they say, sources that they interpret in the light of the debates in modern societies. This study ranges from the Arabic language to the Qur'anic texts, to the practices of the faith, prayers five times a day and fasting during Ramadan. This simultaneously archeological and disciplinary study of Islam seems to them necessary to reconstitute themselves as Muslims, in their faith and in their behavior. Once again, religion is not a fixed category, a ready-made identity, but is instead continually called upon to produce a repertory of ethical and aesthetic conduct. The existence of oppression by the community and of religious conservatism cannot be denied; but neither can we deny that Islam is becoming a point of personal and collective attraction for those who are experiencing secular modernity. The Islamic veil worn by schoolgirls illustrates the personal and aware appropriation of Islam, which often conflicts with the Islam of their parents, which is surely more discontinuous with religious traditions. The headscarf is worn by girls who are much more integrated into German, French, or Dutch society than their mothers, who do not know European languages or the behaviors of communication and exchange in public. Their mothers prefer the affective comfort of remaining with each other, wearing the traditional shawl (and not the headscarf, like their daughters), which goes unnoticed in public. This headscarf, which is traditional and even peasant, was not disturbing when worn by immigrant women because they wore it within the closed space of immigrant communities, marginal people, workers. The schoolgirls, on the other hand, move in public places, share the same spaces, the same language, the same codes of conduct and communication, with non-immigrants. The Islamic headscarf is visible, publicly, and thereby becomes a "problem," a public controversy, as soon as there is the spatial transgression of moving from the periphery into the center.

The presence of Islam raises the question of difference in the most central domains of contemporary European culture, especially in the domains of the body and sexuality, of memory and space. European culture was disturbed and transformed by the counterculture of the 1960s, which reformulated the definition of the subject emancipated and cut off from religious morality. Since then, the feminist and "gay" movements have made the private, sexual, bodily domain a subject of public debate (beginning with the right to abortion and extending to homosexual marriage). The European publics now consider equality of the sexes and sexual freedom as part of their customs and common way of life. Islam challenges the emancipatory perception of the subject and introduces another notion of the feminine subject that is simultaneously public and pious. The presence of Islam in Europe also reveals the secular foundations of the organization of public spaces, as is shown by the magnitude of the debate about the headscarf and its prohibition by law, independently of the different notions of secularism and the public sphere in France and Germany.

The question of how to live together is connected with the notion of space. In the European intellectual tradition, space is conceived of through the notion of the public sphere, or more precisely through the German notion of *Öffentlichkeit* developed by Jürgen Habermas. Historically, the emergence of the public sphere is connected with the process of forming nation-states. However, in the globalized context in which we now live, and more particularly in that of European integration, the notion of a public sphere is of increasing interest insofar as national borders are weakened by transnational forms of communication, by the diversity of linguistic communities, by the fragmentation and the heterogeneity of public spaces. We cannot view the European public sphere as a simple extension of national public spheres. On the other hand, the emergence of Islam in the European public sphere and the conflicts concerning the cultural values of modernity to which its presence gives rise demand an intercultural and even inter-civilizational approach to the public sphere. Such an approach can capture the transversality of relationships between Islam and Europe, because the latter is the place where the encounter takes place, even if there is rejection, confrontation, and violence. A process of interpenetration between Islam and Europe underlies the new, transnational dynamics of the European public sphere. The notion of interpenetration implies a mutual transformation, but it also refers to the existence of force and violence in the area of matters of the body and sexuality.

Finally, Turkey is the major factor in this encounter, and this is emphasized in this book and in the films of Fatih Akin. As a country from which immigration flows into Europe and as a candidate for admission to the EU, Turkey destabilizes Europe's imaginary borders, the borders of inclusion and exclusion of cultural and religious difference. Turkey experiences within itself dynamics that are apparently contradictory: on the one hand, it emphasizes its attachment to secular values; on the other, it testifies to the appearance of Islam through the ethical and aesthetic representation of new urban, educated classes. The public visibility of Islam is symbolized by the Islamic headscarves worn by female students at the universities and is politically propagated by the popularity of the AKP (Justice and Development Party), which has brought to the presidency of the republic a man whose wife, for the first time in the history of the Turkish Republic, wears the Islamic headscarf. This is a spatial transgression, an "invasion" and an occupation of places that had previously been reserved for the republic's secular elites, like the schools, the parliament, and the government. Turks who fear that they will lose what they have achieved in matters of individual and sexual freedom, that they will be dispossessed of their secular power, and who feel invaded and threatened by the arrival of new, religious middle classes and by their political popularity, have sought to erect barriers by means of prohibitions that range from banning the headscarf from universities to banning the party now in power. They attempted, through the medium of a "judicial coup d'état" (March 31, 2008), to break with the democratic contract, to burn the bridges with "the other Turkey" in the name of secular modernity.

The return to nationalism and an authoritarian secularism seeks to impose the hegemony of the *doxa*, which had been challenged by those expressing themselves against the denial of ethnic and religious diversity and against forgetting the past. The taboos on the memory of the Armenian genocide constitute an identity-related complex that folds the Turkish consciousness back on itself. Today, those who are working to end the silence, amnesia, and denial, to connect the present with the memory of the past, are threatened by this return to nationalistic hegemony.

The assassination of Hrant Dink (January 19, 2007), the spokesman for the Armenian cause in Turkey, marked a turning point that has tested the conscience of Turkey as well as its democracy. Dink, who founded the Armenian newspaper *Agos*, which has been published since 1996 in Turkish and in Armenian, had succeeded in doing the impossible—making the Armenian voice heard beyond the limits of his community, giving it an audience even within Turkish society. He worked incessantly to end his country's collective amnesia with regard to the Armenians, recalling their tragic and painful history, the deportations, massacres, genocide, and exile. His battle was less concerned with legal terms or the official recognition of the genocide than with the necessary work of memory to be done, emphasizing the close connection between Armenians and Turks, their common history on the same territory, and the cultural bonds between them. His was a long-term battle, since the Armenian question had been not only repressed in the collective memory, denied by the official history, but also "stolen" by its exportation and appropriation by Europe and the United States. Hrant Dink, through his presence in Turkey and his Armenian name, linked history to the present but also transmitted the heritage of the Armenian past and its tragic events, in which so many lives and families had been destroyed. He did this without compromise and also without hatred. But by publicly denouncing the stigmatization of the Armenians, of which he was also the object, he collided not only with the Turks' violence and rejection, and with the suspicion of Armenians in diaspora, but also with the silence of the Armenians of Turkey. His words put an end to the long discretion of the Armenian community, the heavy comfort of a national amnesia, by giving the Armenian question and a new place in public life.

The public presence of Hrant Dink in Turkey was the symbol of the opening up of the Armenian question, which, in its formerly "marginal" status, was and remains at the heart of the Turkish collective consciousness. That was clearly shown by the very numerous reactions and demonstrations after his assassination. Dink had said in an interview not long before his death that "for Armenians, the best antidote to hate was to live with the Turks." It was not for nothing that he had established his Armenian newspaper in the heart of Istanbul, in the Osmanbey neighborhood. He had created, by the strength of his personality and his convictions, a group of close friends bound together by intellectual affinities and sharing ideas that over time had been transformed into a new school of thought. Hrant Dink was shot in front of the offices of his newspaper, and afterward this place spontaneously became a place of meditation and it was where people gathered for his funeral. A headline in a German newspaper best illustrates the meaning of Dink's death for Turkish society: "One dead, seventy million wounded."

"Part of us died with him," wrote some Turkish journalists, while others emphasized everyone's responsibility for his death. Article 301, under which he had been prosecuted by a group of ultra-nationalist attorneys, and then found guilty, could not leave the political class, the deputies in parliament, or the relays of public opinion untouched. Hrant, whom his trial designated as a special target for racist attacks, felt himself more fragile, more vulnerable. His assassination in broad daylight, in front of his newspaper's offices, in the heart of Istanbul, is an image forever engraved on the collective memory. By a kind of telescoping of the past, that is, with the events of 1915, Hrant's death is an admission, a proof of the countless victims who were killed before he was,. a proof that this time was undeniable but also an unacceptable act. His assassination was felt intimately, personally, affecting every individual conscience as if politics and history had come together in the present and shocked people's hearts. This examination of Turkey's conscience that Hrant had so much desired during his life began with his death. The spontaneous gatherings in front of his house and his newspaper office, the 100,000 persons who took part in his funeral, fulfilled his dearest wish. "We are all Armenians," "We are all Hrant Dinks" said the banners carried by the crowd of young people and old, of all political persuasions, in Istanbul and many other cities. Hrant Dink, a man of conscience, lived on in the heart of his fellow citizens.

Hrant Dink refused to limit the Armenian question to a simple identity-related demand, instead constantly connecting it with questions of democratization and freedoms in Turkey. He was assassinated at the very moment that, in the recent history of Turkey, the Armenian question represented a new stage to be passed through in order to have more democracy. He was killed as taboos were beginning to fall, that Turks, even those belonging to minority groups, were beginning to carry out the work of memory and took up the Armenian question as their own. The Turkish people's spontaneous demonstrations denouncing his assassination expressed this connection, which is now indissociable, between the Armenian question, the relation to the Other, freedom of expression, and democracy. By saying "We are all Armenians," the demonstrators showed, by performing it, the possibility of transgressing identity-related rigidity in order to begin a process of recognition and reconciliation.

The question of how to live together represents a challenge for social stability and democracy in Turkey, but its meaning goes far beyond the borders of this country. Might the Turkish experience prefigure the possibility of constructing a bridge between two worlds? Can crossing and passage between the two be maintained without erecting barriers and burning bridges? Or, on the contrary, is Turkey becoming a microcosm of the clash of civilizations? A terrifying question whose fate and consequences are not limited to local dynamics but are echoed beyond national borders and that concern the future of Europe.

This is a question that tests Europe's capacity to open up its horizon, to conceive itself as a place of mixture and pluralism and not as a mono-civilizational space. This book testifies, not without pain, to this process through which Europe has "alterized" Turkey, emphasizing religion, cultural difference, and its non-membership in the group of nations called "civilized" in order to challenge the legitimacy of the Turkish candidacy for admission to the EU. Turkey has played this role of catalyst, for which it was not prepared, by opening a defensive debate about European identity, on its Christian foundations, on its geographical and cultural boundaries. The Armenian question is very likely to become a "hostage" of this process of distancing with respect to Turkey. European "Turko-skeptics," including intellectuals, politicians, and citizens, on the right and on the left, are seeking to break the "contract," carrying out legal "ploys" and introducing new laws (like those calling for a referendum or a "privileged partnership" instead of admission as a full-fledged member of the EU). The notion of "civilization," clothed in universality throughout the nineteenth century, has changed its appearance and takes on, in the present conflicts, a strangely particularist and mono-cultural look.

The antagonism and competition for control over the European space are not played out exclusively in terms of the market and power but also in cultural terms. Art provokes public controversies, changes imaginations, destabilizes representations of the self and of the Other. It can become a translator between cultures, between different languages and subjectivities, and also, on the contrary, simplify meaning, provide stereotypes, and deepen antagonisms.

Shortly after the fall of communism in Poland in 1989, Krzystof Czyzewski admitted that he found himself in an empty space. Suddenly, the communist state he had opposed no longer existed. This poet, along with a few friends involved in avant-garde theater in Poland, decided to undertake a journey, a long and difficult journey to the east, toward a borderland between Poland and Lithuania, Sejny, where the inhabitants speak several languages, are of different nationalities, and pray in various places of worship. They wanted to "craft a bridge" on this land that would be organically anchored in the soil and connected with social reality and the various strata of memories. In building this bridge, they could not skip over painful questions about the past, the war, the Holocaust, events that were falsified and denied by the communist rulers. Through their efforts as men and women of the theater, they achieved a work of memory with the participation of the inhabitants of Sejny.

At its best, the theater is an exemplary public space, a space that is built like a bridge and makes possible an encounter and mixture of peoples, memories, and cultures. *The Sejny Chronicles,* or the oral histories of the multicultural city of Sejny, became a play recognized throughout the world. In 1990, Czyzewski created the Borderland Foundation in order to promote his project in other multicultural regions of Europe, like the picture of the Old Mostar Bridge that appears on this foundation's webpage; a bridge that connects the two banks of the river Neretva, where the roads between the Ottoman Empire and Christian

Dalmatia met. Moving beyond identity-related rigidity, transgressing the homogeneity of spaces, becomes a stake for all intellectuals, artists, and politicians who see themselves as builders of bridges between different temporalities, memories, and cultures.

CHAPTER 2

Contemporary Islam

The difficult task is to become one's own contemporary.
—Marcel Gauchet, *La Condition Historique*
Paris: *Stock,* 2003

Islam is becoming the contemporary of the modern world. Although simple, this observation is in no way facile, for it is accompanied by a process of confrontation that challenges the modern world's way of seeing things. The entry of Islam onto the stage of history has not always followed peaceful paths, any more than it has followed a logic of assimilation to the Western world. The ways in which it is becoming contemporary are sometimes anachronic with respect to the foundations of modernity, and they do not leave Western societies and their self-images undisturbed. The encounter between Islam and modernity has led to a mutual transformation and at the same time blurred modernity's points of reference. Proximity and distance: this book will reexamine this twofold movement of attraction and convulsion.

It is in Europe that we can best observe this encounter; there it is staged in individual practices and in public debates. Islam situates itself in this space in different ways and is thus becoming a European question. In turn, European identity is increasingly disturbed, challenged by the presence of Islam. We must therefore focus on this zone of contact and confrontation in order to study the relationship between Islam and Europe. Should we adopt a more transversal, performative point of view in order to show how the process of exchange is transforming both Islam and Europe? But in this exchange, certain unexpected effects escape the actors and their intentions. These effects represent something unprecedented in social experience, and thus produce history. This essay's ambition is to grasp this shadowy side of social experience, these ongoing processes that are neither completed nor, a fortiori, archived—in other words, to seek out, behind the snapshots of the present, the designs of history. It is a way of thinking about history through certain events, in the fragments of the present. But how can we determine the meaning of events before they have been sorted out, archived, and identified by time? How can we distinguish the significant amid the trivial and ephemeral?

The task is made all the more difficult by the fact that the modern way of seeing things seeks to preserve its monopoly on the definition of civilization, its initial control over the universal. How in fact can we move beyond the cognitive order to which the narrative of modernity belongs? We have to decenter the European view, adopt a twofold European and Muslim point of view, in order to break this framework and get past the mirror of the modern consciousness. We have to carry out sociological work that involves simultaneous translation of intercultural practices, work that takes place between, in the interstices, in the zones of contact and confrontation. What are we looking for, if not the inaudible, deviated meaning that is "lost in translation"?[1] Thus the voice of the sociologist, instead of masking itself in the name of an alleged scientific objectivity, will make itself heard—as Clifford Geertz urged[2]—in such a way as to introduce intercultural reflexivity.

Becoming contemporary

September 11, 2001, clearly revealed the violent eruption of Islam at the heart of Western hegemony. This date marks a new stage in globalization, not only for Islam, but also for the United States, which had up to that point been spared the devastating effects of this phenomenon. Thus Islam showed itself to the world as a contemporary: rejected as "medieval" and "obscurantist," it resurfaced in contemporary life. From that time on, it has established itself as a "problem" for conceptions of the world. The Islamist phenomenon, which has been in gestation since the beginning of the 1980s and which, moreover, cannot be reduced to terrorism alone, is no longer limited to the Mideast or the Arab world. It no longer concerns only Shiite Iran or secular Turkey, but circulates among contexts, acquires a transnational dynamics, and establishes itself in Western spaces, in *die Weltzeit*.

Although globalization means that parts of the world that used to be distinct, separated by time and distance, are now approaching each other spatially and synchronically, a primary characteristic of the current encounter between Europe and Islam[3] is the fact that it is undergirded by the structures and networks of global communication. The synchronization of the event also produces perverse effects, misunderstandings, collisions between different publics. From September 11, which was experienced live and on the global scale, to the photos of American soldiers in the Abu Ghraib prison and the videos of hostages in Iraq, all these phenomena testify both to the constitution of a global public and to collisions among various publics, leading to their mobilization in war and terrorism.

Unlike other periods, in which the relation between Islam and Europe was governed, as in the case of colonialism, by geographical distance, but also by different temporalities (the one being "more advanced" than the other), our age testifies to the simultaneity and proximity of experiences. Nevertheless, this experience of proximity is lived on both sides in a way that is as disturbing as it is blinding, and makes contemporaneity difficult or even unbearable.

This is because contemporaneity is not a simple chronological experience of the present time but rather an experience of recognition. Extending beyond the field of interpersonal relations, it is not immediate, given; on the contrary, it has to be constructed anonymously. Paul Ricoeur, reflecting on the articulation of individual memory with the collective memory, emphasizes the variations in the relationship between self and other. Thus appears the question of proximity as a dynamic relationship to be accomplished and constructed: "to make oneself close, to feel oneself to be close."[4]

Islam's contemporaneity with the Western world involves the question of proximity. It is by becoming contemporary with the Western world that Islam reveals its anachronic relation to modernity. Its actors assert their presence in Europe through religious markers such as references to the sacred, the practice of rituals, and wearing religious insignia in secular and profane places. Contemporaneity and anachronism are linked to the expression of power relationships between those who appeal to contemporaneity as exclusive power over modernity and others who do not identify with this Western experience of modernity and assert their anachronic difference as a rejection of the expression of domination. Thus both Europe's "denial" and non-Westerners' "rejection" underlie the power relationships between "central" countries and the rest. Postcolonial critiques, including "Subaltern studies"[5] in India and the Islamist revolution in Iran, can be seen as a rejection of assimilating modernity by means of a resolute strategy of anachronism. But in the European context, where the comfort of distance has been lost and where practices are synchronized, the question of proximity arises with great intensity. In Europe, more than in any other part of the world, the question of contemporaneity with Islam appears as a crucial question, a question on which Europe's own development depends; for it is there that this conflictual encounter manifests itself as the proximity of Europe and Islam.

A structural production of proximity and simultaneity is connected with the social experience of Muslims and Europeans; the colonial past (and also the impact of the history of the Ottoman Empire, which people have far more trouble recognizing[6]), migrations, and, more recently, globalization, have contributed to the interweaving and connection of human practices. Thus it is difficult or even impossible to speak of distinct civilizations;[7] modernity was transmitted as a vector of the secular social imagination (of equality and freedom), took form in institutions (such as the nation-state, the parliament, civil society), was standardized by the market economy (and its corollary, consumer society), and ended up acculturating peoples very distant from the center of modernity. Today, globalization is accelerating circulation and multiplying the networks of connection between different parts of the world, men and women, publics and markets. The differences that are emerging do not proceed from outside the global system but from inside, and even from inside Europe. European countries are experiencing the presence of Islam within themselves and are faced by the question of cohabitation.

The new old bridge

The story of the destruction and reconstruction of the *Stari most* ("old bridge") in Mostar, Bosnia, marvelously told by Michael Ignatieff in his book *Kaboul-Sarajevo*,[8] provides clues for understanding the complexity of the Muslim presence in Europe, of the Ottoman heritage in the Balkans, and the long-term memory that shapes present conflicts.[9] In 1566, at a time when the Ottoman Empire's control extended as far as Budapest, an engineer named Hayreddin, a disciple of Sinan, Suleiman the Magnificent's master architect, came to the city of Mostar to construct a bridge over the Neretva in order to symbolize Ottoman imperial authority and to connect the mosques and markets on the two sides of the river. Over the centuries, the beauty of this bridge won people's affection, and it became an icon of the city. Ignatieff tells how he himself saw it for the first time when he was a little boy, during a trip with his parents from Belgrade to Dubrovnik via Sarajevo and Mostar. It was in Sarajevo that he first visited a mosque, the great mosque in the center of the old city's bazaar, and realized that there were Muslim Europeans, and had been for centuries. The *Stari most* also made a great impression on him. He writes that it was "built of beautiful old white stone, arched over the tumultuous blue waters, and seemed to be of an incredible delicacy, too slight to bear the weight of a man or a horse." But this bridge had stood up to all burdens, both physical and symbolic. Remaining after the Ottomans were driven out of Bosnia in the 1890s, it survived the First World War and the conflicts between the Serbs and the Austro-Hungarians, as well as the battles fought by partisans during the Second World War. In Tito's Yugoslavia and during the 1960s and 1970s, it began to enjoy a certain fame: tourists came by bus from all over Southern Europe to see it. It was in 1992–1993 that madness gripped the residents of Mostar: Muslim and Croatian militias, whose members had been schoolmates, had become enemies and shot at each other for eighteen long months, in house-to-house fighting. On November 9, 1993, a Croatian artillery unit destroyed the old bridge. A video made by an amateur shows the bridge collapsing into the river. "When a bridge is destroyed, there usually remains, on one side or the other, a kind of stump. At first it looked to us as if the bridge had collapsed without leaving anything behind, taking with it part of the rock, the stone towers that overlooked it, and clumps of Herzegovinian earth. Later we saw that on both sides there were real wounds, open and bleeding," wrote Predrag Matvejevic, a writer born in Mostar in 1932.[10]

At that point, the international community helped reconstruct the *Stari most*, which bore a very heavy symbolic weight: a bridge between the past and the future, between the Croats and the Muslims, between Bosnia and the international community, between the Muslim world and Europe.[11] Its reconstruction was intended to contribute to the "spectacle of reconciliation" after ten years of division between Croats, Serbs, and Bosnians. But the man who was chosen to rebuild it was neither Muslim nor Croat, but a French engineer, Gilles Péqueux, who had, moreover, never seen the bridge before its destruction. Perhaps it is no accident that a French engineer trained at the school of *Ponts et Chaussées* created by Napoleon was assigned the task. We might, in fact, point out, as Ignatieff does, that engineers played as important a role for the sultans in Istanbul as they did for French kings and emperors. A symbol of Ottoman influence in Europe, the *Stari most* also attracted the attention of Turkish government agencies and the businessmen who participated in its financing and reconstruction.

Europeans, Turks, and Bosnians hastened to reconstruct the bridge at Mostar as if it were a matter of course, in order to recuperate a piece of history, to do away with scars, to avoid mourning. Thus the inauguration of the new bridge, on June 23, 2004, became a spectacle of reconciliation, a subject for the proliferation of political metaphor that, according to the architect, compromised the reconstruction project itself. Returning an old bridge to the contemporary world, creating a "new old bridge," is in fact no easy task. For Gilles Péqueux, the project was more located in the act of reconstruction itself; it takes time to study in depth what the predecessors had in mind, without making the reconstructed bridge either a copy or an imitation: "The idea was to get into the state of mind of Hayreddin, a Turk who arrived with two or three other Turks and about thirty people from the region. What has to be noted is that in the Orient people cut stone differently from the way it is cut in the West (which for this purpose extends as far as Venice). What is moving about this work constructed in the sixteenth century is that it is more a kind of collective sculpture than a classical work of art. I say collective sculpture because the beauty of the work consists in the fact that it is a set of errors corrected by a mixture of Oriental and Occidental know-how. In a way, Mostar is the place where the East and West joined hands."[12]

The events in Bosnia may have been early omens of the tragedy that is beginning to play itself out today all over Europe: it is there, in the heart of *Mitteleuropa*, that the Europeanness of the Bosnian Muslims has been put to the test. In 1995, during the Bosnian conflict, whereas the Serbian government conducted a policy of destruction and ethnic cleansing directed against Muslim and Croat groups in Bosnia, the European political authorities remained inert, letting the American military do the work. Without the initiative of certain French and American intellectuals (like Susan Sontag) who tried to "get close" to the Bosnian people, European public and political opinion might have remained indifferent, or even showed some reluctance to recognize Slobodan Milosevic's policy of ethnic cleansing for what it was.[13] The political documentary film produced in 1994 by Bernard-Henri Lévy and Alain Ferrari, *Bosnie!* appeared like a cry of indignation directed at international public opinion but also as a glance at Europe itself. The film ended with the expression of the hope that "Europe did not die at Sarajevo." As a kind of "little Europe," Bosnia thus became the metaphor for the destruction or reconstruction of Europe. Jean-Luc Godard's film *Notre Musique* (2004) formulates the same hope and explores the reconstruction of the bridge in Mostar and of Sarajevo as a metaphor for a potential reconciliation on the global scale.

The new old Europe

In fact, the question that arises in today's world is whether Europe can represent a place of reconciliation, a common space, a project for the future, when it has to deal with the stakes currently involved on the global scale. How can the new old Europe be constructed without falling into the labyrinths of the past, on the one hand, or the denial of what is now at stake on the other? In other words, how can old Europe become its own contemporary? It is old like the bridge at Mostar; and like this bridge, it wants to be constructed as a place of circulation and reconciliation. So far as that is concerned, we can only agree with Ignatieff when he writes: "There is some irony in the fact that Europe wants both to keep the Turks out and to rebuild this bridge, which is a symbol of its multiculturalism and of the Muslim heritage."[14]

The destruction of such places as well as their reconstruction shows the battle being waged today over symbols and the power relationships that underlie them. Unlike the bridge at Mostar, the void left by the two World Trade Center towers remains to this day unfilled. The reconstruction project continues to be a subject of controversy among architects, promoters, elected officials, and families of the victims. "Ground Zero" has become a place where political and emotional stakes are involved. The families of victims demand more space for the memorial, the residents of the neighborhood do not want to live with a cemetery in the middle of their community, and the promoters and financiers on Wall Street try to dictate the laws of the market. Once again, as was already the case for the bridge at Mostar, the project of reconstruction has been compromised by its symbolic freight, its emotional charge, and the pressure put on it by political and financial powers. The project's architect, Daniel Liebeskind, who made his name with the Jewish Museum in Berlin (2001), seeks to connect memory and hope, in the spirit of his earlier work.[15] The question he asks is how to build on the basis of tragedy, how to perpetuate the memory of the dead while at the same time looking toward the future and delivering a message of hope. With the "Freedom Tower," which is intended to be more than a commemorative edifice, Liebeskind imagined a "common space" including the symbols of democracy. The Tower is to be 1,776 feet high, a direct allusion to the date of the American Declaration of Independence, and to be topped by a spire alluding to the Statue of Liberty's arm holding the torch.[16]

Ground Zero continues to be a battleground for various actors, including Muslim residents of New York. A decade after 9/11, a plan to build a mosque near Ground Zero provoked controversy. A columnist for the tabloid *Washington Examiner* expressed his anger, seeing the plan as "the second attack on the World Trade Center."[17] It is argued that erecting a mega-mosque near the site of massacres would wound the families of the September 11 victims. On the other hand, the American Society for Muslim Advancement defended the project as a chance to allow moderate Muslims to differentiate themselves from terrorism and help build a pluralistic public life.[18]

However, conceiving of, imagining, and building a common space, sharing the symbols of traditions and trajectories different from those of the Western world, is not an easy undertaking. Since the Iraq war began, a fracture has appeared between two Wests—America and old Europe (particularly France)—putting in question the common space and work, and diverging in their definition of freedoms and of what is called "Western democracy." We must not underestimate the power relationships and rivalries within the West for the appropriation of memory, of the places and symbols of modernity. The Twin Towers mirrored the height of commercial and financial exchange networks' will to exercise global control, whereas the bridge at Mostar, small and splendid, symbolized a site of intermingling, a zone of contacts and exchange across cultural and religious frontiers. The taxonomies of places and symbols and their inscription in global memory are being hierarchized.[19] In fact, memory is becoming a site of competition for access to the universal and the global. There is no "just memory" but only "the disturbing spectacle provided by too much memory here, too much forgetting elsewhere."[20] The destruction of the Twin Towers instigated a new world (dis)order of which they are the foundations, and 9/11 has become the memorial date of this world-making event. From the point of view of European history, the destruction of the bridge at Mostar and ethnic cleansing in Bosnia were no less significant. However, these latter events have not been remembered with as much zeal; they have not acquired the weight of a date and have been almost abandoned to oblivion. Is that already a sign that the European project is collapsing? Europe, like the bridge at Mostar, is modest in size but the bearer of enlightenment from one bank to the other, on both sides of civilizational borders; after having reached its apogee, has it now become too old to face up to the new world, caught between America on one side, and Islam on the other? The ancient character of the European heritage, which is the source of its wealth, seems to weigh too heavily and to stand in the way of Europe as an idea and a place, as an influence, as a project of "making a world."[21] Only such a project will allow European countries to move beyond national experiences into a common space and time and think about the question of European development.

Europe's confrontation with American power, on the one hand, and Islamic dissonance, on the other, presents a challenge to the European project that imperils it. The referendum in which the European constitutional treaty was defeated, first in France (55 percent against, May 30, 2005), and then, three days later, in the Netherlands (62 percent against), revealed a hiatus between the rise of national feeling and the European project.

Countries as different as Holland and France, one guided by multiculturalism, the other by republicanism, have shown the same concern to defend their own values and the same rejection when confronted by the intrusion of Islam into their symbolic system and their everyday life. In considering the alteration of the European area, we must not underestimate the impact of Islam. It is not an accident that the two countries that rejected the adoption of the constitutional treaty by means of referenda are those in which Islam is the object of intense debate. The question of immigration and that of the Turkish candidacy for admission to the European Union set the agenda for public debate about Islam. The presence of Islam in Europe, conveyed by the immigrant population or borne by the Turks' desire to join Europe, appeared to the European consciousness as a forcible intrusion, undergone and not desired, provoking a feeling of losing the bearings of its identity, its geographical and cultural borders—in short, as an invasion. The sense of being "at home" seems to have been affected by the presence of Muslims in Europe.

The Islamic terrorist attacks carried out by Al-Qaeda in the heart of cities like Istanbul (November 15 and 20, 2003), Madrid (March 11, 2004), and London (July 7, 2005) merely strengthened this sense of confronting an "enemy within."[22] Although the transnational aspect of terrorist networks is clear, the identity of the perpetrators of the suicide attacks stupefied people in Turkey as well as in Spain, and, more recently, in England. The perpetrators of the attacks in London did not come from other countries, but were British citizens of Pakistani background, born in England, and had led rather quiet lives, even being well-integrated into British life (one of them worked in his father's fish and chips shop, a sign of his adaptation to British tastes in food; another taught in a school for handicapped children, which could be taken as a sign of his humaneness). What led British Muslims preoccupied with life in their neighborhoods, their families, and their jobs, to allow themselves to be won over to a "jihadist" mentality characterized by hatred and destruction? This question, an important one, remains unanswered. But behind these acts we can glimpse a religious community, a transnational *umma*, independent of national origins, a Muslim jihadist category that is not limited to Arab Muslims, and does not spare British Pakistanis, thus transcending every national, regional, or confessional borderline. That is what is revealed by the close interweaving of this transnational Islam and its inscription on European soil.

The assassination of Theo Van Gogh (November 2, 2004) revealed the violent modalities of this inscription. As an intellectual figure, Van Gogh personified the freedom of speech and provocativeness dear to Dutch tradition. His murder by an immigrant from Morocco, for a film he had made about the condition of Muslim women, had major repercussions and triggered a debate regarding the limits of the tolerable. The event showed the cluster of problems involving immigration, Islam, the gender question, and the confrontation with European norms. Van Gogh's film, entitled *Submission*, was produced with Hirsi Ali, a member of the Dutch parliament who was also known for her critical positions regarding Islamic religion as a source of female subjection. She herself, a refugee of Somali origin, had succeeded in transgressing the borderlines of her community of oppression and had thus become a spokesperson for the emancipation of Muslim women. The production of the film by these two figures with such divergent personal trajectories, who differed in religion and gender, gave concrete form to the proximity, encounter, and intersection of these two worlds. But this intersecting path was not able to avoid what it condemned: violence.

The film's message is simple: Islam inflicts cruel practices on women. It begins with a prayer and tells the story of four women who tell God about their suffering, the abuse to which they are subjected to by men: forced marriage, incestuous rape, domestic violence, lapidation for adultery. Showing images of women wearing transparent robes and with verses from the Quran written on their bodies aroused reactions. For some critics, the film did not avoid caricaturing Islam, with the result that it degraded Muslim women.[23]

The translation of intercultural experiences is not without perils: it easily leads to a telescoping of meaning and a collision between different audiences. In the European context, Muslims find themselves led to reflect on their status as a minority and their connection with non-Muslims. The question of gender, the status of women, is central to this reflection. Whereas the European definition of citizenship is based on the question of gender and sexuality, the assassination of the film producer revealed the repertory of dissension, showing how difficult it is for two systems of values—freedom of speech and women's liberation on the one hand, the rejection of blasphemy and the sacralization of women on the other—to engage in negotiation and debate. At the same time, the clash, even if violent, has intensified the inscription of Islam on the Dutch public consciousness—literally, because the incident took place on the streets of Amsterdam, is registered there, stained by blood and claimed by the terrorist in a letter written in Dutch and addressed to the Dutch public.

Nevertheless, we must avoid adopting too binary a view of Islam and Europe and inquire into the place of religious norms and liberal values in Europe.[24] In France we can point to the prohibition in 2005, at the request of a Catholic group, of an ad for a brand of stylish clothing.[25] The ad campaign was inspired by Leonardo's *Last Supper*, and showed a single man, the Apostle John, seen from behind and wearing only a pair of jeans, while Jesus and the other apostles were represented as women dressed in designer clothing. This inversion of the sexes was trying to be a wink to Dan Brown's best-seller, *The Da Vinci Code*, in which the author asserts that in the fresco showing the Last Supper, the person sitting at Jesus' right is not John, but Mary Magdalene. The creators of the ad sought to provide a new representation of the Last Supper for commercial purposes by giving the power to women, substituting for Jesus and his apostles women parodying the attitudes and gestures Leonardo painted. This ad campaign was banned on the ground that it offended Catholics' religious feelings. Such a prohibition shows the complexity of the interconnections between the sacred, the symbols of the religious, the inversion of sex roles, women's bodies, and the laws of the market and desire. And beyond that, it shows that the questions that made the actors of Islam emerge on the frontiers between the sacred and the market, the religious and culture, sexual modesty and sexuality, are not external to modernity, to European development, but on the contrary are close to the roots of more fundamental questions about the ethical, aesthetic, and scientific definitions of the subject and his or her body. Questions bearing on sexuality, abortion, homosexual marriage, and the artificial uterus all demonstrate that Western societies are increasingly disturbed about human control over life and death, by shifting borderlines between nature and culture and between moral prescriptions and individual choices and freedoms.

The terrorist attacks have produced differing repercussions in each country, but it is in these zones of contact and confrontation that Europe is taking form or falling apart. The Istanbul attacks forced political authorities to acknowledge the existence of a terrorism that was religious in origin, and to condemn it. In a country with a Muslim majority, the difference between two forms of Islam, one at war with Europe, the other pro-European, has grown significantly deeper. The Madrid attacks led to a change in political leadership and the withdrawal of the Spanish military presence from Iraq. Unlike what happened in Spain, in England the presence of the British army in Iraq was mentioned only timidly, while the strengthening of anti-terrorist laws was given priority. Spokesmen for British Muslims were congratulated for having straightforwardly condemned the terrorist acts committed in the name of Islam, proving their allegiance to the British citizenship. Paradoxically, these acts made more explicit the European character of the Muslim presence, but not without provoking new forms of ethnic and religious discrimination. The buried memory of the "Balkanization" of Europe may be causing an upheaval in the collective consciousness and challenging the "new old Europe."

Places, publics, politics

The presence of Islam within Europe concerns the sharing of the common space, whether defined as the public sphere where debate takes place or as the European space where a political idea is emerging. Thus terrorist acts as well as the different forms of Muslim visibility are directed toward this space and invade it. Islam's actors, who are immigrants or the children of immigrants, are reterritorializing themselves in European spaces, challenging the values that underlie Western ways of life. The attacks strike the spaces of urban life, namely public places (streets, railway stations, subways, busses), meeting places (cafes, discotheques), places of trade and travel (markets, shopping centers, hotels)—in short, all the places where a social link is created and the individuals involved are constantly changing.[26] The murder of civilians is a murder of the city, an "urbicide," to use Monique Canto-Sperber's expression, which strikes at the physical reality of the city and its cultural meaning.

It is in the public space that the presence of Islam is displayed. Terrorist attacks, the affair of the Islamic veil in France, and the controversy over Turkey's candidacy for admission to the EU are problems that differ greatly from each other yet are connected and amalgamated in the common consciousness and in public memory. Terrorism targets the public first of all and is situated outside the field of political negotiations; the veil is emerging as a personal statement, first of all in the schools; the Turkish candidacy, which was initially considered in the domain of foreign relations, has quickly become a matter of domestic politics. These different aspects of the Islamic presence in Europe are treated, when they appear in the debate, as political and legislative problems. Legislating on security, the banning of religious insignia in public schools, and the referendum on the European constitutional treaty (which has been transformed in part, in both Holland and France, into a referendum on the Turkish candidacy) are symptoms of the translation from public authority to political and juridical decisions.

The public sphere, as I have already said, is the stage on which the drama of the encounter between Muslims and Europeans takes place and where this intersection reconfigures the nature of the public sphere in turn. The latter is not a fixed, pre-established structure: on the contrary, it changes like a theater set with the arrival of new actors who present new ways of living, communicating, and living in it. The intrusion of Islamic actors into the European public sphere transforms the situation. The republic and its laws have of course put their stamp on the public space. But the res publica also signifies an autonomous space where unprecedented practices and problems can emerge and be expressed. Only totalitarianism seeks a perfect agreement and correspondence between the public space and the republic. There are, in fact, nondemocratic republics. A society's democratic force is defined by its ability to make public the problems that arise and to make itself the contemporary of the "other's" problems. Pierre Vidal-Naquet has studied these problems of democracy in the Greek city-state by using the concept of the "social elsewhere": the study of women, slaves, foreigners, and other groups excluded from participation in the politics of the city-state enabled him to understand its central core.[27] For the early modern period, the central focus of Michel Foucault's work was the ways in which the insane, the sick, criminals, homosexuals, etc., were excluded from society. But how can we deal with other forms of exclusion in our contemporary democratic societies, especially if we take the whole world into consideration?

The approach to the modern public sphere proposed by Jürgen Habermas highlights the connection with contemporary democracy. According to him, public deliberation and discursive practices are the means that allow the functioning of democracy as an ideal type. The public sphere is the site par excellence of rational political exchanges between responsible citizens. But it seems to me that more than rational deliberation, it is an emotional substrate that underlines the spectacle of the encounter between Islam and Europe. The notion of a public space appears here in a concrete sense, as if we were dealing with a stage on which a spectacular tragedy was unfolding. Both suicide attacks and different modes of religious action in everyday life put into practice a dramaturgy of disparate and even contradictory religious repertories. Various interpretations and representations of Islam in the modern world compete and fight with each other. But here there is also challenge for Europeans, who must translate their perilous encounter with Islam into a political project.

It is in the public space that this encounter takes shape. It is the site of an Islamic performativity, for terrorists and for any other kind of religious action, ranging from the wearing of vestimentary insignia to respect for religious rites or the invention of modes of consumption and leisure for believers. It is the place where the Muslim presence not only manifests itself but also affects awareness and elicits debate among members of the European public. A certain difficulty in understanding and giving a name to these practices persists. This difficulty in naming illustrates the fact that people find themselves confronted by unprecedented practices for which there are not yet any words. What should we call the religious aspect of contemporary practices? Or the role of modern political thought in contemporary Islamism?[28] Terrorist or martyr, war or jihad, the veil worn by a Muslim woman or by a Catholic nun, religious or political signs, European or Asiatic Turkey—in all these cases, the difficulty lies in drawing and defining borderlines, placing the cursor between the political, the cultural, and the religious. But in each case, the religious amplifier operates in the European public to make still more alien what is already alien.[29] To understand the conflictual but close connection between Muslims and modernity (which can be formulated in a double affirmation and/or by a double negation—Muslims and moderns or neither Muslims nor moderns) is not a simple matter for either Europeans or Muslims themselves. For Muslims, this entails giving up their aspiration to a total Islamic identity. As for Europeans, they have to rediscover what they have in common with the other and thus give up European "purity."

In sum, the entry of Islam into contemporaneity is taking place through fragments and anachronic relations with modernity. Europeans experience the presence of Muslims through a series of events that are not necessarily connected with each other, but which appear in the public eye in disparate forms.

Islamic fragments: an expressive movement

I am not talking, then, about Islam as a homogeneous entity, a "civilization" that is intact and impervious to historical change. But neither can we limit ourselves to talking about the plurality and diversity of Islam. Today, Islam is becoming less a faith than an ethnic, cultural, and political reference point for Muslims who live in the spaces and experiences of modernity in Europe. Islam is becoming a movement; we can speak of religious action insofar as Islam is subject to a discursive and performative interpretation on both the personal and the collective levels. Notions such as "radical Islamism" and "neofundamentalism" seek to account for Islam's political and collective activation. But the approaches adopted by political scientists emphasize the collective and ideological aspects of the movement, without taking into account the problematic and personal relation to modernity. On the other hand, Muslim actors are not lagging behind modernity; on the contrary, they make use of modern technologies and tools of communication; they have mastered the language of politics and become familiar with urban life; they invest in the market and adjust consumer products and leisure sectors to conform with the new needs of religious groups. In short, they do not deny themselves the use of the tools of modern life. But the use they make of them remains religious.

Moreover, contemporary Islam is not conveyed by actors exterior to the system but rather by actors who are the bearers of modernity: young people, women, cultural intermediaries,[30] entrepreneurs, the middle classes. These actors have learned the techniques of public representation, manipulate the terms of political debate, and know the rules of the market. They display their religious difference in common spaces, in schools, universities, hospitals, businesses, and in parliament, but also in places for recreation and vacations. Thus they challenge the fundamental values of European public life such as secularity, the equality of the sexes, and freedom of expression. The fact that Islam is becoming public means that Muslims are asserting and displaying their presence and their religious difference in the pluralist framework of European publics.[31] This leads to the invention of different Islamic public spaces, "heterotopies" or "counter-spaces" in which Islamic actors work out their religious identity through performative acts and collective rituals.[32]

The exacerbation of this public and religious visibility distinguishes the contemporary Islamist movement from earlier ones. This visibility is conveyed in the public space by various modes of religious action, including personal and bodily performativities. Thus there is a subjective and expressive aspect to Islamic religious action and not a single political trend with a revolutionary aim. But the "expressive"[33] nature of Islamic action is underestimated and even misunderstood, because expressivity is associated with a process of emancipating the subject and self-realization, that is, with creative and progressive action. It is in fact difficult to classify Islamism as a creative and progressive social movement in conformity with the Enlightenment narrative. But it would be too limiting to restrict the study of human action to its progressive, creative, emancipatory version alone. Islam is transformed by human interpretation and action; there is thus a particular connection between action and religion. The presence of the Muslim religion in action cannot be understood as a purely political instrumentalization. On the other hand, Muslim action is not identical with other collective forms of social action and social movements. We have to bring out the distinctiveness of Islamic religious action. I would therefore emphasize the fragmented but expressive aspect of Islamic action. There is a linguistic and corporeal expressiveness. The notion of expression characterizes a process in which something internal is externalized and becomes perceptible; religion is recalled as a repertory of action, circulates as a social imagination, and thus exteriorizes and inscribes itself on the body and in space.

This is why the figure of the veiled woman and the figure of the martyr, even though they are opposed, elude any approach or explanation in terms of the instrumentalization of the religious and of the rational and collective logic of political action. Nevertheless, these two figures are presented as icons of religious action. These two icons of Islamism are presented without political mediation and without organizational or institutional representation. Seeking to define "a new paradigm,"[34] Alain Touraine shows the primacy of the cultural domain and the absence of representativity as characteristics of the contemporary world.

In these two figures, the "expressive" aspect is important. The veil is part of the elaboration of a feminine religious performativity and of putting a collective Islamic imagery into circulation. But above all, it is a personal and bodily appropriation of a stigma (the veil signifies female subjection, according to the narrative of modernity). It expresses the externalization of this stigma as well as the will to invert it and make it a sign of power and distinction for women. Religious prohibitions and values of sexual modesty work on the subjectivity of this femininity in opposition to emancipatory femininity. The difference of the body's techniques creates a disharmony between the emancipated female subject and the religious female subject. A conflictual "intercorporeality" is expressed with respect to the veil. Between these two figures of woman a battle over "civility" and "civilization" is being waged because the relationship to the body becomes the pivot for the debate about the cultural orientation of modernity and customs. The Muslim woman appears as the marker of an insurmountable alterity between the world of the civilized and the world of the barbarians. The *Mona Lisa* wearing an Islamic veil published on the cover of *Time* magazine[35] can be interpreted as illustrating this dangerous conversation, as the close interweaving of the veil and Europe, and especially as the expression of a threat to the icons of European modernity.

At the other extreme, the "martyr" figures display a destructive capacity of religious action. By scorning the values of life, the human body, and urbanity, they accept Western civilization's way of seeing Islam as inferior. They transcend through barbarism the taboos of civilization and urban life. We may also note that the Turkish word for "civilization"—*medeniyet*—is derived from the word *medina*, which means "city" in Arabic. The destruction of cities signifies the destruction of modern and civilized modes of life. (But didn't the much-admired British composure with regard to the London attacks express the English people's determination not to change their way of life and their civility?)

It is clear that neither the veiled student nor the terrorist martyr are conforming either to religious orthodoxy or to popular traditions. On the contrary, these "active minorities"[36] characterize an exit from institutional religion and reflect a process of acculturation and entry into the experience of global modernity by participating in the elaboration of an Islamic social image repertory. Thus we are not dealing with problems that are "minor" or "false" for the majority of Muslims who live peaceful lives, nor with epiphenomena of political Islamism. In fact, the question of the veil has often been treated as secondary, seen as proceeding from political radicalism and as an instrumentalization of women by men. As for terrorism, it has been described as a matter of networks, and thus limited in its capacity for recruitment. It has also been analyzed as an admission of Islamism's inability to mobilize support and thus as its last gasp. At most, it has been seen as a product of the West. Perhaps such a denial of Muslims' agency and subjectivity is sought as a therapy for the West's endangered hegemony and as an optical illusion to dissimulate a disturbing proximity.

These fragments are zones of encounter that crystallize a set of problems and conflictual conversations between Islam and Europe. They constitute the nodes of this encounter. It is a matter of an interpenetration (in the biological sense, but also in the sense Niklas Lühmann gives to this term[37]), because there is a bodily, sexual, and also forced, even violent aspect to this communicational encounter. Muslims force their presence within Europe. The Turkish candidacy and its desire for Europe are seen by Europeans not only as suspect but also as an intrusion across the geographical, historical, and religious borders of Europe. The Islamic veil is disturbing because Muslims express their difference by "ostentatious" signs and thus force people to see them. Finally, terrorism is an affirmation of Islam by "apocalyptic" means. But if the Turkish candidacy and the Islamic veil express a process of mixing and cross-fertilization, establishing a connection between Muslims and Europeans, suicidal terrorism expresses a will to annihilate oneself and the other. It is an admission of impotence in the sense that it manifests the inability to endure the interpenetration of Islam and modernity.

This is not an encounter between two distinct systems, two "civilizations" that are supposed to be different and separate, but rather of an encounter through zones of contact. We can trace the advance of this process in "snapshots" of it. The veil, the suicide attacks, the Turkish candidacy are all fragments of this history. They are also indices of the fragmentation of Islam and of the plurality of its interpretations or of its modes of religious action and dialogue with Western civilization.

Ever since Islam appeared, there have been conflictual presuppositions about what it should be. Two traditions emerged, the Shiite and the Sunni, leading to a "cumulative dialogue" of response and counterresponse.[38] But the contemporary dramaturgy is written in an intercultural conversation and on a civilizational disagreement. The Islamic drama is not written in purely religious terms, but as a response and counter-response to the cultural program of Western modernity.

Turkey is a major part of this inter-civilizational conversation, because since the abolition of the caliphate[39] or Ataturk's introduction of secularism—as today with its desire to join Europe, which is also expressed by a political power that has emerged from the Islamic movement—Turkey has represented a major stake, not only for the European world, but also for the Muslim and Arab world. Turkey, as the "bad Muslim" allied with the Western world, has been ignored if not despised by the Arab world. It has won some respect in the eyes of Arab nationalists for its refusal to support American policy regarding the war in Iraq.[40] The Islamists are perplexed by the rise of a power alternative to their interpretation of Islam, and Iranian reformers are closely following the democratic experiment being conducted in Turkey.

It is on the basis of these anachronic but contemporary fragments, Islamic but European, that I seek to understand the recurrent patterns of this encounter. The force of evil and passions are not absent; on the contrary, they are intrinsic to it. As Monique Canto-Sperber reminds us, what is up front "in the new condition of the world [...] are the passions aroused by the comparison of oneself with others. These passions range from envy and resentment to a blind will to destroy."[41] The very minimal difference in proximity elicits comparison and triggers passions; the fear of invasion by the other, the loss of oneself and one's home underlies this encounter.

The encounter between Islam and Europe has not taken place without being accompanied by a feeling of losing purity and authenticity. By erecting barriers based on cultural identity, Muslims and Europeans both seek to overcome the feeling of loss that they experience in the presence of the other. For Islam, to the extent that it establishes itself as affirming its cultural identity, the modern world is becoming unbearable. On the other hand, when Europeans affirm their culture and their identity as a civilizational identity, Europe as a project suffers. We have to remember that the French eighteenth-century positivist conception of civilization, which was adopted by the Ottomans, had the immense advantage of making the West appear in secular garments rather than Christian ones.[42] Today, the notion of civilization seems to be more a matter of cultural identity than of a secular universalism.

Fixations on cultural identity increase, by a kind of mirror-effect, the alterity of what is already other: civilized and barbarian, emancipated and subjected, European and Muslim. Making the other different again in order to create one's own identity is a way of blinding oneself in the mirror of the other, of falling prey to illusion and destroying any possibility of finding common ground, of constructing a link between the self and the other. It is in a situation in which the comfort of distance no longer exists that we have to rethink a space that might bring people together. The stake for Europe is not the recognition of Islamic difference, but on the contrary the ability to rethink and reconstitute a common place between the two and to move beyond the conflictual dialogue. This requires both sides to move beyond fixations on cultural identity. Muslims, who constitute a religious minority in Europe, must learn to live with other religions.[43] Anti-Semitism, which goes back to the heart of Europe, is the cursor of these inter-religious relations whose political importance is growing.[44] Europe is simultaneously haunted and roiled by this past. Thus the European character of Turkey is tested by the recognition of the Armenian genocide. It requires moving beyond Turkish nationalism based on forgetting its multireligious and multiethnic past. The European perspective can ease this work or, on the contrary, block it, if the hegemonic and identity-based narrative of Christian Europe prevails.

Does Europe define itself as an identity or as a political project? For most Europeans, there is natural continuity between the two. However, the rejection of the European constitution revealed the tensions between identity-related and nationalist fixations and the construction of a transnational project. The tacit equation between the heritage of the past, the Christian religion, and the European project has become explicit when confronted by the Islamic presence in Europe. Without being too pessimistic, one can say that in light of recent events, Europe as a project, as the invention of a political connection, of something in common with the other, as the production of a universal, as a way of making a world, has been slowed if not halted. In order to get it going again, two keys are required and a double point of view has to be adopted. As in the reconstruction of the ancient bridge at Mostar, it is necessary to find common ground between ways of doing things, between civilizational differences, in order for bridges to hold up, to connect peoples, religions, and continents. Thus the question of Europe, like that of civilization, is not reducible to political will, to the staging of spectacles of construction or commemoration. It has to be conceived as a kind of "constituent assembly," and "something like a 'people' and like an 'idea' has to be given."[45] In short, it has to be conceived as grafting.

A political grafting that can be achieved only by using intellectual tools of thought but that must take into account the devastating emotional and tragic aspects. It does not lend itself to a smooth narrative in terms of interaction, intercultural dialogue, and cohabitation between cultures. It involves a process of interpenetration, or even a quarrel inscribed in the body, in the memory, and in space. We cannot become contemporaries of each other without disputes, without enduring anachronies, or accepting that there will be discords.

CHAPTER 3

The Terrorist Moment

I was driving down the little hill (*Aşiyan*) of the Bosporus with my assistant Uğur, who is working on a study of the new Islamic cafes in Istanbul as meeting places for Islamists.¹ We were talking about the new forms of visibility that Islam is acquiring in the secular public space when my cell phone rang. It was my niece Zeynep, who works in the financial sector and is constantly connected to the Internet (keeping up with the sectors and temporalities of the globalized word, like most young Turks of her generation). She told me what had just happened in the United States. At that moment, one of World Trade Center towers had just been hit. I drove home as fast as I could and watched, almost live, the attack on the second tower. For hours, even days, I remained petrified in front of the television, switching from CNN to TV 5 and the Turkish channels. I looked in vain for the words that would give meaning to the images, a narrative that would explain this tragic event. The incessant and repetitive flow of images created a hypnotic effect and conferred on them a kind of autonomy, as if they were impregnating my mind directly through the senses, without passing through the intellect.

The moment, momentary images

As I have just done, we begin by seeking to use words to reconstitute a personal narrative of the moment we have experienced. Individuals from all sorts of backgrounds and living in various places have resorted to memory to arrive at a meticulous description of where they were at the moment of the attack, what they were doing when they learned of the attack, and how they reacted. As if by remembering their experience at that moment they could understand the meaning of the event. Through the repetition of images, the circulation of personal narratives, that moment was registered in our collective memory.

Similarly, when there is a declaration of war, an earthquake, or someone dear to us suddenly dies, a fracture line is created in our memories. We remember the moment, just as we remember a date. Time is divided into before before and after.[2] Americans call this dividing line 9/11; in Arabic, date and history are designated by the same word: *tarih*. September 11 has become a historic date.[3] (Or should it be considered instead a historic end, like a new calendar announcing the end of progressive modernity?)

In any case, we have had the feeling that we are entering (or burying) History through a private door. This history was written in capital letters by personal narratives.[4] History and everyday life were joined in a single moment, almost in real time. The moment of terrorism was experienced personally, but also simultaneously and globally. September 11 combined, not without clash and discomfort, people who were separated by time, place, and culture. The juxtaposition of images of New York and Kabul, of George Bush and Ben Laden, formed a kind of disturbing and surreal collage.[5]

The historical moment is remembered as a montage including both images and people's stories.[6] September 11, the image whose narrative we have been trying to work out ever since imposed itself on us. At first, terrorism had neither a name nor a voice. Like New York: mutilated and mute. Stopping time, stopping life, as if someone had hit the pause button. We participated passively in this historical moment, as if watching a film or rather a video clip without sound. The catastrophe was accompanied by silence. An absence of demands from the terrorists, an absence of spectators' stories. Those who were in nearby skyscrapers watched from behind their double-paned windows as the towers collapsed, while those watching their TV or computer screens were viewing terrorism live. Terrorism was displayed, under glass, and the transparency of the glass allowed us to witness, dazed, our own impotence. History as the ability to act and to create a narrative was challenged.[7] The sole heroic act was that of the firemen, who were dramatically transformed into involuntary martyrs (like a kind of reverberation of the terrorist martyrs).

September 11 was graven on our memories by images far more than by words. We watched, we witnessed collectively the collision of the airplanes, the collapse of the towers, the fires, the falling bodies. Far more than by rumor or words, it was by visual violence that the event held us spellbound and that terrorism was spread on a global scale.

However, despite the unprecedented nature of the event, the arguments put forward gave little attention to the rupture that it constituted and took refuge in the past or projected themselves into the future. People usually situate themselves either before or after this event. Either they try to find the reason for it in the past history of American policy and the Soviet invasion of Afghanistan or in cultural differences (the clash of civilizations between Islam and the West); or ethical arguments are brought against terrorism and war or in defense of freedom and peace. But there have been few reflections based on the description of the moment, very few attempts to understand based on the instant and the image, on temporality and the visual, that is, on the terrorist moment.

To create a narrative, we have to return to the moment and the image and rethink the event as a snapshot, a *Momentbild*,[8] an *image momantanée*. We have to pause on the image, look at it, enlarge it, examine the details, and free it from the grasp of the past and the future.

Islam and modernity

It was only when the second tower was struck that the source of the attacks was revealed and the names of Ben Laden and Islam were associated. At that moment I heard myself saying that it was impossible that this was the result of Islamic terrorism. An attack of such magnitude seemed to me so excessive, so much on the American scale, that it could not have been imagined by Muslims. Furthermore, the extensive technological expertise, meticulous organization, and long-maintained secrecy that these attacks presupposed did not seem to me typical of Islamic activism. Like many other people, I was convinced that Muslims were not capable of perfectly executing such a complex action.⁹ In addition, during the first hours after the attack, the France-Press news agency mentioned the name of a Japanese terrorist group, a rumor that seemed to me plausible, given the Japanese kamikaze tradition and the necessary technological mastery, Hiroshima constituting a motive for vengeance. After the terrorist attack in Oklahoma, we had been greatly surprised: the alleged Muslim terrorists turned out to be in reality very "ordinary" Americans. Obviously, this refusal to recognize Islamic terrorism showed that I was in denial, because for me such a recognition signified a threefold defeat. There is no neutral audience, and I speak as part of the audience most directly concerned, as a Muslim from the Middle East and especially as a researcher seeking to put into perspective the nonviolent intersections of Islam and modernity. But this denial did not reflect solely an intellectual and political defeat. My arguments, like those of many others, regarding Muslims' inability to undertake such an action ultimately expressed a feeling of inferiority that this attack sought precisely to invalidate, as I was to understand only later on.

September 11 forces us to rethink the relations between Islam and modernity. The terrorists benefited from theoretical and practical training in the United States and in Germany. They were able to take courses, travel, and live in Western countries without attracting attention, passing themselves off as ordinary citizens. Not only had the terrorists familiarized themselves with the modern world and lived in proximity to it, but they were also products of it. We cannot say that they were excluded from modernity. They did not turn against the "shock" of modernity, against its occupying, exogenous power. On the contrary, we can say, at the risk of seeming cynical, that Islam and modernity have never been so close as they were in the moments preceding their collision and simultaneous annihilation, which the planes' double attack on the towers symbolized in a tragic way.

The division and proximity of two worlds (rich and poor, countries speaking in the name of human rights and countries subject to authoritarian powers, societies in search of happiness and societies deprived of a future, civic societies and corrupt societies, the market of libidinal consumption and populations confronted by famine) create a destabilizing gap that can lead to wounds, feelings of victimization, injustice, revolt, and a thirst for revenge. But structural causes and long-term reasoning do not suffice to understand September 11. Causal arguments can certainly help us understand the social seedbed in which such terrorist acts take root. We can extend endlessly the list of objective causes, but that just moves us still further from the terrorist moment by making us forget the intrinsic motives and by trivializing the connections with Islam. And when this objective will to achieve a historical and causal understanding of the event is coupled with a good intention—not to reduce Islam as a religion to terrorist acts—the event moves even further away. The terrorist moment becomes secondary. It is no more than an epiphenomenon.

On the one hand, arguments that are difficult to refute, such as "Ben Laden is a product of American policies" or "we have sown the seeds of our own destruction" testify to this concern for historical objectivity over the long term, as well as to a critical perspective with regard to the West (and still more with regard to the United States).[10] But this view nourished by the West is two-edged: claiming to be critical and investigating its own responsibility, it nonetheless thereby attributes power to itself and still sees itself as the sole master of historical action. It is, of course, comforting to think that the world is still ruled by the West.[11] But September 11 changed Muslims' self-image, roles were reversed, the West's vulnerability was made clearly apparent, the Americans became victims. People continue to think in terms of the habitual schemas, as if this terrorist moment had not taken place. To be sure, we are still in a phase of re-establishing power relationships by means of war, which has in turn produced new victims in the Muslim world. But September 11 has given Muslims a feeling of power, even if it is mediated by evil and destructive forces. Even if this unavowed feeing is not translated into terms of political power, it participates in the production of a new collective Islamic self-image.

A new Islamic self-image

The September 11 attacks revealed this self-image that had silently taken shape, independently of national or community differences, like those between Saudi Arabia and Iran, for example, or between Sunnis and Shiites. Among the indications of this evolution that culminated in September 11, 2001, we can mention the taking of hostages at the

American embassy in Tehran (1979), the fatwa issued against Salman Rushdie by Khomeini (1989), and the Taliban's' destruction of the Buddhas of Bamiyan in Afghanistan (2001).

Each attack creates a new political, or rather metaphorical and "metapolitical," icon, and acquires a new Islamic religious resonance with jihad, martyrdom, blasphemy, idolatry, and usury (or financial capitalism, which the World Trade Center symbolized). A whole forgotten side of the Islamic idiom was reactivated in a new context, in an antagonistic relation with modernity. This lexicon is used (and misused) to give meaning to these political "meta-actions" and to arouse a collective memory of Islam. In a world that prizes tolerance, individual freedom of expression, multiculturalism, and art, people want to recall, and even impose, the religious borderlines between the permissible and the prohibited. The Islamic lexicon is connected with a feeling of belonging to an imaginary Islamic community (*umma*). But it suffers from syncretism and popularization.

The Twin Towers and mimetic desire

The targets on September 11, the Pentagon and the World Trade Center, are in this context symbols of the two faces that America presents to the outside world: military power and financial capitalism. But it is the attack on the Twin Towers that has become the image and the symbol of diabolical destruction: the airplanes that gutted the towers, the fires, the trapped people jumping from the windows, the collapse of the towers, the number of human lives lost, the bodies that were never found—all these facts caused a visual and ethical trauma in the collective memory.

The weapons (the airplanes) as well as the targets (the Pentagon and the skyscrapers of the WTC) chosen by the terrorists represented the two technologies of the industrial era that have facilitated human mobility, the exploration of the globe, and urban concentration. Going as far, as high, and as rapidly as possible—these have been the goals of technological innovation. Today, by comparison with the advances in the technologies of communication, we can say that skyscrapers and air transportation are no longer great novelties. We have gotten used to not being astonished by them—up to September 11, when airplanes and skyscrapers suddenly became hostile inventions.

By their transparency and solidity, the Twin Towers, constructed of steel and glass, were considered a symbol of modern architecture. They crystallized arrogance and genius to transcend the limits imposed by nature and geography. For their architect, Minoru Yamasaki, there was no limit to height: "It doesn't matter what height you reach. [...] What really matters in Manhattan, is the space occupied on the ground."[12] The Twin Towers had become one of the icons of New York.

The architecture of these towers gave no hint of their use. Their transparency did not make it possible to see into the offices or discern their human occupation. Thus on September 11 the towers collapsed before our eyes without death being visible. Only an abstract figure, indicating the number of victims to be between 3,000 and 5,000, gave us some idea of it. The bodies had simply disappeared in the flames, the metal debris, the shards of glass, and the ruins. People tried to make up for this absence of bodies by publishing biographies of the dead every day in the newspapers.

According to Eric Darton, whose book on the Twin Towers was written long before September 11, the mind of the builder of the towers and those of the terrorists shared one characteristic: in both cases, undertaking creation or destruction on such a scale involves conceiving human life and social life at a very high level of abstraction, which in turn leads to a feeling of domination.[13]

The profiles of the victims and those of the terrorists also present similarities: both were in their thirties and were high-tech. But unlike the victims, the terrorists did not share in the joys of daily employment. Two kinds of arrogance thus collided, one that was defined by construction, science, and work, the other by destruction, religion, and death.

Violence and purity

But there were two towers and two destructions. The attack on the Twin Towers involves a phantasm.

Doubleness inspires fear;[14] the phobia regarding twins in traditional societies is well known. Physical resemblance is considered enigmatic, baleful, because the erasure of differences raises the problem of classification, of the contagion of the same and the impure, as René Girard reminds us. And all impurity leads to the eruption of violence. The relation between violence and sexuality is the common heritage of all religions, and twins are impure in the same way as women and menstrual blood.[15] And it is to violence that all forms of impurity (blood, one and the same substance, is both what soils and what purifies) must be subjected.[16]

September 11 was the expression of a quest for purity by way of an absolute terrorist action, an attack on the most "evil" symbols of the West. For terrorist martyrs this quest for purification is also a personal quest. A manuscript provides minute details of the religious instructions and practices to be respected to ensure that the final mission will be successfully carried out: "Review the plan, check your weapon, adjust your clothes so that they cover the private parts of the body, pray, purify your soul, cleanse yourself of any stain by removing any hair and sprinkling your body with eau de Cologne." Mohamed Atta's will, written well before the attack, reveals his obsessive fear of being soiled by sexuality and contact with women: "The man who washes my body around the genitals must wear gloves in order that they [the genitals] not be touched"; he demands that his body be dressed in "new clothes made of white fabric" and that "no pregnant woman, no impure person" be authorized to say farewell to him before his burial; similarly, "no woman must be present or, later on, come to weep over his tomb."[17]

The phobic fear of women and twins are one and the same response when confronted by resemblance and the impure. It is similitude that poses a problem for the Islamist man of today. Modern societies are governed by the implementation of resemblances, similarities. The aspiration to an egalitarian, democratic society has as its consequence the erasure of borderlines between men and women, young and old, nature and culture. Religious and cultural certainties based on natural boundaries (geographical, biological) are shaken. Woman is the pivot of this transformation, symbolically and corporeally. The more she crosses the boundaries of the private space, of the biological, of the "natural," the more she blurs the differences between private and public, cultural and natural, feminine and masculine.[18] The interchangeability of roles, clothing, and even genders is made commonplace by modernity. And the modern world, which prizes hybridizations and cross-breedings,[19] does not cease to grow, to clone itself, to propagate itself on the planetary scale (we find, for example, a "World Trade Center" in every large city in the world). And the Muslim world is no exception. On the contrary: Islamism is a symptom of all this.

This similitude and the increasing proximity of the modern world and Islam, of men and women—therein lies the whole question. It is not the "clash" of difference[20] and some kind of distance but on the contrary proximity and similarity that are the origin of the anxiety. Islam, including that of the Mideast (with its physical proximity to Europe, monotheism, and emigration), illustrates in the most dramatic way possible the problematics of the "little difference."

Islamism is far from being loyal to religious traditions: its discourse, simplistic and anachronistic, is based on references to the Qur'an taken out of context. It produces an amalgam of different popular traditions, national cultures, and religious schools. The return of Islam is carried out by misappropriating religious traditions, both texts and *ulemas*. The authority connected with the interpretation of the text of the Qur'an undergoes a democratic erosion. Thus jihad can be declared by a man without any religious authority, whose legitimacy is based solely on his activism.

Nor are the actors of Islamism "purely" religious. They are mixed products of modernity. Two central categories of actors, Islamist engineers and veiled female university students, indicate this hybrid, crossbred character, insofar as they amalgamate rationality and faith, the veil and education.[21] September 11 was the conjoint result of the presence of engineers and the absence of the veiled students. The alliance between the Taliban and Ben Laden shows this fear of modernity and of women. The Taliban movement is the most fanatical expression of this phobia. It represents the most radical attempt to imprison women in their bodies, to push them back into their inner space. The violent quest for purity leads to a flight from women and from modernity.

In other words, Islamic modernity can be written only in the feminine.[22] On the one hand, the Islamic veil represents the will to define and preserve the difference between men and women, private and public, Islam and modernity. But on the other hand, Muslim women are investing the spaces of modernity, acquiring public visibility, mingling with men in mixed places. This paradox plays a pivotal role in the orientation of the Islamist movement in general, as well as in that of women in particular. Its recognition opens up a field of critical reflection and creative conflictuality. Ignoring it leads on the contrary to dogmatism and destruction.

The main question for Islamists and for the Muslim world in general is how to reconcile themselves to their own modernity. While thinking they were expressing their radical anti-modernism, the Islamists of September 11 made manifest their own modernity and the dead ends to which their rejection of this modernity leads them. By destroying the most disturbing symbols of modernity, the "neo-martyrs,"[23] actors at odds with the Muslim world, have destroyed their twin. They have mutilated themselves, just as they have mutilated their women. They have left the Muslim world mourning for modernity. However, by a perverse effect, September 11 has pushed Islam more than ever toward the front of the stage. Since then, Islam has not ceased to be part of the dynamics of globalization. It is around Islam that public debates, exchanges of ideas, books and newspaper articles are organized. We recall how the sales of the Qur'an increased after the event, as if one could understand the meaning of the event by referring to the text of the Qur'an. In any case, caught up in a global dynamics, Islam and the Western world have never been so close. September 11 revealed their proximity and contemporaneity.

CHAPTER 4

The Istanbul Attacks and Islamic Scenography

In November, 2003, Islamist terrorism struck Istanbul in a series of attacks. The first time, two synagogues in the city center were targeted by suicide attacks with car bombs. Five days later, on November 20, the same scenario was repeated: two targets were hit simultaneously, by suicide attack with car bombs. This time two powerful explosions damaged British buildings, the British consulate, and the HSBC bank.

Why was Turkey chosen as the site of Islamist terrorism? How can we explain qualifying terrorism as "Islamist"? Or what is there that is "Islamic" in terrorism? Do people mean thereby to point to a link with religion or to the politicization of Islam? Or does terrorism have neither a religion nor an ideology, representing only a degraded form of politics, or even the end of politics?

I put forward the hypothesis that if Turkey has become one of the sites of global terrorism, that is because it is a central stake in the competition to represent Islam on the global scale. What was targeted was precisely what it represents: another face of Islam, different from the one advocated by Al-Qaeda and by the partisans of the thesis of the clash of civilizations. It is this alternative Islam, which has a human face and can accommodate European values of political pluralism and secularism, that these attacks sought to destroy. But Islamist terrorism cannot be summed up in an act of barbarism and destruction. Confronted by the modern world, it also seeks to restore or reinvent a religious repertory establishing prohibitions and boundaries that designate the enemies of Islam. Thus instead of drawing a distinction between terrorism[1] and religion, or seeing in the former the instrumentalization of the latter, I will try to explain how religion is recoded and reintroduced into the political agenda by an Islamic terrorism that operates on several scales, local and transnational, and that addresses several audiences, national, religious, and Western.

Political explanations of the Istanbul attacks have for the most part focused on the events that preceded them. Thus the war in Iraq and the agreements for military cooperation and exchanges of high technology signed in February and August 1996 between Israel and Turkey were given as the main causes for the choice of targets. Specialists in Islam have moreover shown that the rise of terrorism reflects a deficit in Islamist politics, illustrating the loss of its political ability to mobilize the masses and to seize power in some state or other. According to this argument, it is the decline of political Islam that explains Islamist terrorism, interpreted as an admission of political impotence. On the one hand, this is a very limited conception of Islamic politics, if it is to be restricted to revolutionary strategies for taking state power. On the other hand, to consider Islamist terrorism, on the model of the leftist terrorism of the 1970s in Europe, as the last hurrah of a political movement that is unable to "re-enchant" people's minds, is far from being able to account for the direction it has taken on the global scale. Since the September 11 attacks, not only has it occupied a central position in the new configuration of international politics, but the questions relating to the presence of Islam in political life, within Muslim countries as well as in Europe, is continually growing in importance in public debates.

Temporality and terrorist moments

Although the message of the Istanbul attacks was addressed to the global audience, they were staged on very precisely targeted sites. Thus we must examine them more closely, at the micro-level of the terrorist event, in order to seek clues on site instead of limiting ourselves to the political and international level. I would therefore like to re-examine the moment of these attacks before putting them into perspective in their historical context. In this way, far from reducing the terrorist act to a blind reaction or even to some kind of admission of political impotence, we will be able to detect the political meaning that its perpetrators sought to "create" through it. In fact, Islamist terrorism participates in the production of religious meaning and seeks to obtain a monopoly on the representation of radical Islam. Beyond the targets chosen, its goal is not merely to demonstrate its ability to destroy, but also to implement a religious repertory that awakens echoes in the Muslim collective imaginary and can erupt in the political space.

Grasping the event as it occurs in the present is what is required by the nature of terrorist acts that appear like a sudden and devastating lightning bolt interrupting the flow of ordinary life. These acts occur in the wink of an eye, in an *Augenblick* as the Germans say, or like a snapshot, as English has it, combining rapidity with violence (*snapshot* was originally a hunting term, referring to a quick shot taken without deliberate aim). Moreover, it is this immediacy that makes terrorist violence something outside real time, anachronic, and quite literally nightmarish. Just as we desire to awaken as quickly as possible from a nightmare, we want to move on to another life sequence, forget the moments of terror, and get back to ordinary life. However, since September 11, this return to ordinary life has become increasingly difficult. Our ordinary lives plunge more and more deeply into the shadow of terrorism. Since then, each attack merely strengthens our feeling of dread; we live with the fear that the world might become a stage on which the actors of destruction might appear at any moment. To be sure, terrorism produces "snapshots," but each one is situated in a process, an overall action, whose development we grasp in an instant. The attacks multiply in time and in new places, on the planetary scale. It is this ongoing process that constantly redraws the map of Islamist terrorism.

The literature on terrorism does not really take the destructive instant into account. The explanations offered by this literature are usually situated in a broader, long-term political context that takes international relations and economic conditions producing inequality and social injustice to be determining. More than terrorism itself, what is studied is the social terrain that prepares the way for terrorism. As a result, we move away from the moment in order to enter into a long-term logic. These analyses thus give priority to a different explanatory hierarchy.

By cutting us off from the moment, they show that they desire a return to ordinary life as much as the citizen does. One of their effects, which is therapeutic, is to encourage us to move on to other sequences in political and social life that are governed by other temporalities. Thus the moment is subordinated to explanations of a more structural and long-term order.

A global landmark for terrorism?

On September 11, 2001, Islamist terrorism created a kind of historical turning point. The attacks on New York and Washington opened a new era, because what we witnessed was a change in the scale of Islamist terrorism. The attack on the Twin Towers has since established itself as the landmark for this new terrorism that is now exercised on the planetary scale. The series of attacks in Istanbul are part of this new logic.

Al-Qaeda's terrorism has struck in similar ways in places as distant from each other as New York and Istanbul: multiple targets, simultaneous explosions, recourse to martyrdom. Terrorism is becoming a global phenomenon in the sense that, no longer limited to a specific country or region, it acts on the dynamics of the international political configuration. The meaning its acts acquire transcends local politics. Thus the Turks had the feeling that they had been chosen as a local target in a game whose scenography was global. Contemporary Turkish history has been traversed by various modes of ethnic, religious, and political terrorism (the Kurdish PKK movement, the Islamist Hezbollah—which has no connection with the Lebanese Shiite movement—and the extreme left movement DHKPC). But the feeling that these latest attacks involved a quite different logic and did not really concern Turkish national politics (even though they also sought to disrupt the latter) was a feeling shared by various observers in Turkey as well as in Europe.

There is a gap between the nature of the event and what it is called. The term *terrorism* cannot easily be applied to these attacks, because it presupposes a politics of demands and a margin for negotiation. Terrorist movements of the nationalist type, for instance, were connected with the defense of a territory or a demand for autonomy. In the case of Islamist terrorism as it was manifested in New York and Istanbul, as in other places, we are confronted by its actors' silence, by an absence of specific demands. One of the reasons that we describe Islamist terrorism as global is this lack of geographical distinction. Terror also proceeds from the fact that we cannot see the aggressor's face or hear his words, while at the same time we have the feeling of being thrown into chronic war.

Illustrating the transnational *umma*

Islamist terrorism is often conflated with the declaration of holy war, global jihad.[2] But this is a war without a state. Although the Americans have tried to target the "axis of evil" by designating states that shelter and order terrorism, terrorist jihad is organized and propagates itself in transnational networks. The West's response to Islamist terrorism generally remains on the national level, whereas Islamism more easily projects itself into the global era through a religious community, an imaginary *umma*. This is well illustrated by the profile of terrorist militants, who come from all national origins. After the Istanbul attacks, Turks were astonished to find that there was a local network. But the recruitment of terrorists of Turkish origin, and not solely of Arab origin, is part of the implementation of a strategy that consists in constructing a terrorist network that illustrates the existence of this transnational religious community.

The Turkish terrorists' itinerary also shows the international aspect of "holy war": they are said to have fought in Bosnia-Herzegovina, then in Chechnya, to have spent time in Pakistan, and then established themselves in Syria and on the Iranian border. But although they belonged to these transnational networks of Islam, the perpetrators of the attacks were not "deracinated." On the contrary, they are Turkish nationals, all from Bingöl, and belong to the same family. Here we see the solidarity of an ethnic, almost tribal base connecting with a technological entrance into global modernity (they owned an Internet café). In addition to its participation in transnational networks, terrorism's ability to arm itself proves that it has entered this global modernity. In the 1980s, Bingöl, which lies in the middle of southeast Turkey, where the majority of the population is Kurdish, was one of the fiefs of the radical Islamist movement Hezbollah. It would seem that the state, before dismantling the organization in 2000, asked it to act as a militia against the Kurdish nationalist movement (PKK). The small groups that continued to exist covertly were able, investigators said, to pursue their clandestine activities but did not have the ability to carry out terrorist actions on the scale of the ones in Istanbul. It was the connection between these groups and a new ideological matrix and their recruitment by transnational networks that gave them their striking force.

In general, Islamist militants are recruited among young people from well-off families, and sometimes even come from a secular and democratic background, as seems to have been the case of the terrorists from Bingöl. According to the town's mayor, parents often do not know that their sons belong to these radical groups. The itinerary followed by Azad Ekinci, who is described by his schoolmates as an ordinary guy who loved soccer and tobacco, and thus was "typical": "His father, a government official and a respected Kurdish militant, had been assassinated by local nationalists when Azad was one year old. He was raised by his mother. Except for school, he and his brother didn't go out much. After high school he enrolled at a university in Istanbul. When he returned three years later, he is supposed to have ordered his mother to wear the Islamic veil."[3]

What causes someone to move from Islamic radicalism to suicidal terrorism? What relationships are there between suicide attacks and Islam? Islamic jihad, which means "the struggle on God's path," can be interpreted in two ways: one warlike and the other personal and spiritual. In the first sense, especially referring to armed battle for the defense or expansion of Islam, jihad is "one of the doors to Paradise" for the "soldiers of God" (*mujahid*); those who die in engaging in it are "witnesses" (*Shahid*) to the faith, martyrs.[4] But the current form of Islamist terrorism breaks with orthodox interpretations of the religion, including the Shiite tradition of martyrdom, because the martyr is a person who dies fighting for the defense of the community, not one who deliberately seeks death. Islamist terrorism adopts the Shiite tradition of martyrdom, connects it with the kamikaze's forms of combat, and extends it to Sunnis. This syncretism is one of the characteristic traits of contemporary Islamist terrorism. The word *terrorist* itself refers to agency, whereas suicide attacks annihilate all mention of their actors—except through their death, their accession to martyrdom, to which they give an unprecedented interpretation.[5] Islamic radicalism involves a certain "bricolage" of religious meaning, a more personalized relation to Islam, that is, one more independent of the interpretation given by religious authorities but also closer to the forms of modern terrorism. The terms *martyr* and *kamikaze* seek to shed light on the profile of these terrorists but do not account for the nature of the action, the targets chosen, or the way various audiences perceive these attacks.

The scenography of the religious

These attacks struck not only their designated targets but also bystanders of all religions and classes, and destroyed whole neighborhoods. The four attacks in Istanbul on November 15 and 20 resulted in 61 deaths and more than 700 wounded. One of the explosions took place near the Neve Shalom synagogue, not far from the Galata tower, right in the middle of Istanbul. The whole façade of the synagogue was destroyed, and in front of the building there was an enormous crater. The other synagogue targeted was that of Beth Israel in the Şişli neighborhood, five kilometers away. This second explosion destroyed part of the British consulate in the historic Beyoğlu area. Following these explosions, the facades of the buildings collapsed. Debris, broken glass, and wrecked cars were strewn all over the streets. Amid these scenes of devastation, residents and passersby moved about in a state of shock, their clothing shredded by the power of the explosions. Fireman sought to extinguish fires that had broken out, while rescue teams took the wounded to local hospitals. "It was like an earthquake," witnesses said. The scenes of destruction resembled those produced by the earthquake that had hit Izmit several years earlier.

The worldwide circulation of pictures of these events created an effect that Ulrich Beck has called the "globalization of emotion."[6] The new technologies of communication disseminate powerful images, thus founding a kind of collective memory. The residents of Istanbul understood the reality of Islamist terrorism by associating it with September 11. "Here it has become like New York," cried a weeping Istanbul resident. This association with September 11 reflects the feeling that these terrorist attacks in Istanbul were not part of a domestic logic but of a foreign one: the establishment on the global scale of an Islamist rhetoric conveyed by attacks on local targets.

At first, the destruction struck us so forcefully that we were blinded by its inhuman, even apocalyptic aspect. The attackers sought to destroy, without limits and without hesitation, human lives, neighborhoods, places of worship, buildings where work was carried on, and historical monuments. The extent of the destruction initially prevented us from seeing what was quietly being set up. Each attack contributes to the elaboration of an Islamic imagination. We can understand the execution of the religious meaning only if we place ourselves at the local level, taking into account the symbols that are put into play.

The attacks on Istanbul's synagogues occurred during the Jewish Sabbath, when the Jews of Istanbul had gathered in these places of worship for the Saturday prayer. In this case, it was not the agreements between Turkey and Israel that were targeted by these attacks, in some more or less abstract way, but rather the very existence of the Jewish community in Istanbul and its freedom to practice its religion. The choice of synagogues was not secondary or accessory but primary. Analyses in terms of politics and international relations shift attention away from what can be directly seen (in this case, the fact that the target was the synagogues and not an official building), and present experience and the emotion (that of the Jewish citizens of Istanbul) as elements of political analysis. But terror is a way of intimidating or even directly threatening not only political decision-makers but also ordinary citizens. The attacks on the synagogues were directed against the presence of the Jewish people but also against that of the Jewish religion in the land of Islam; and thus they represent a menace both to the heritage of the multi-denominational Ottoman Empire[7] and to the presence of the Jewish community under the secular republic. The terrorist act is a kind of training, a performance, a simulation of a break with Ottoman history and the secular republic that creates a *tabula rasa* in order to implant a different conception of Islam. Al-Qaida's terrorism opposes the heritages of Islam in order to put its stamp on a "virgin" space. The goal is to intimidate the Jewish people of Istanbul and keep them from practicing their faith, to make them feel that they are not at home there, and to remind them of the religious dimension in a secular country. The desire to destroy the synagogues is part of a desire to prevent the practice in the land of Islam of any religion other than the Muslim religion. Radical Islamism seeks to control the public space and to clothe it in the hegemony of the religious.

The choice of British targets in Istanbul has been explained by Turkey's alliance with America and with England, even if ultimately Turkey is not involved in the war in Iraq. Of course, this war may have played a crucial role in the attacks, and especially in the choice of the British consulate as a target. I have no intention of contradicting these arguments; instead, I want to draw attention to another, less apparent factor that operates at a deeper level of the Islamic memory and imagination. The attack on the HSBC bank targeted less "British interests," as part of the international press quickly asserted on the ground of the bank's British origin, than "interest" itself, the usury (*faiz*) practiced by the banks and a whole generation of young Turks who have been trained to work in these sectors of international finance. The perpetrators sought to reaffirm Muslim law, which prohibits the system of bank credit; but instead of participating in the legal battle within Islam regarding this subject, they made a direct attack on the icon that incarnates lending, the bank itself. Once again, we see how Islamist radicalism slides from textual and literal protest into symbolic protest and figurative destruction. Thus terrorism proceeds to reintroduce a religious repertory. If the latter in fact depends on simplifications and cuts itself off from Muslim theological knowledge, that makes it easier for it to enter into circulation on a collective and popular level. We are dealing less with an ideological construction than with the fabrication of an Islamic imagination staged by religious terrorism.

Thus we find here again a mixture of political icons and the religious register. The Iranian Islamic revolution was accompanied by the application of Sharia; Khomeini's fatwa against Salman Rushdie symbolizes the condemnation of blasphemy; the Taliban's destruction of the statues of Buddha in Afghanistan targets idolatry; September 11 in New York and the declaration of a "global jihad" can thus be considered to be among the "signposts," to borrow the title of Sayyid Qutb's book,[8] that serve as a point of reference for radical Islamism. A date and a place correspond to each icon, and thus each participates in the elaboration of a kind of cartography and also of an Islamic imagination.

Rather than in the domain of ideology, which remains concentrated in the hands of a relatively limited number of intellectuals, terrorism acts on this aspect of the religious imagination that feeds on collective images and representations. Each offensive act elicits an echo that seeks to conquer new territories (the *futuhat*) and new images by reactivating certain prohibitions when confronted by a world that prizes not only human life and freedom of thought, but also pleasure, religious pluralism, and secularism. Terrorism redraws, in a virtual, imaginary, and theatrical way, the borderlines between the Islam that it advocates and the modern world that it condemns.

The terrorist act, in its alleged unity, corresponds to several layers of superimposed and mixed meanings. We can grasp in the moment itself this synthesis that the terrorist act carries out, but we can also grasp it through the accumulation of indices of which this moment is composed and that realize the association, at first invisible, of political and religious meanings. Furthermore, these strata of terrorist action are not perceived and hierarchized in the same way by different publics, European, secular, and Muslim.

Islam with a human face

Turkey, which is simultaneously secular, Muslim, and pro-European, constitutes in itself a privileged audience, a choice site for Al-Qaeda's terrorism.[9] What this organization targeted, then—and here I return to my first hypothesis—is another face of Islam represented by Turkey, which is not the one advocated by Al-Qaeda and all those who preach the doctrine of the clash of civilizations. Islamist terrorism seeks to destroy this alternative Islam with a human face, the Islam of an open society, of Turkey as a hyphen between two civilizations. Terrorist Islamism wants to blow up the bridges that connect Turkey not only with the West, but also with other Muslim countries. It seeks to cause the failure of a local experiment that might acquire exemplary value for these countries and a more universal scope. In fact, even more than the model provided by the Iranian Islamic revolution, the experiment being carried out by the Party of Justice and Development (AKP) is being closely watched by various Muslim publics. The AKP, which emerged from the Islamist movement and has been in power since the general elections of November 3, 2002, takes credit for the transformation of the Islamist political movement into a "conservative democratic" party. It distinguishes itself from both groups that advocate terrorism and from those that take the Iranian Islamic revolution as their model. Its policy is openly situated in the heritage of Turkey's secular and pro-European republican heritage. It was under this government that a series of reforms were adopted that sought to harmonize Turkish laws with those of the European Union: the abolition of capital punishment, the lifting of legal obstacles to free expression, the teaching of local languages, including Kurdish, new legislation dealing with Christian foundations, and finally the limitation of the influence of the military (the National Security Council) in political life. These reforms show how the European perspective works in Turkish political life, creating a legal framework and giving rise to a process of democratization endorsed by the AKP government.

This government also gained credibility among the publics of the Arab and Muslim world by refusing, in March 2003, to involve Turkey in the Iraq war. This refusal marks a turning point in its alliance with the United States, though it has not attracted the sympathy and support of the European political powers, which remain very skeptical with regard to Turkey. But the AKP government's noninvolvement in the Iraq war has brought it, without this outcome having been sought for its own sake, an Islamic legitimacy that Al-Qaeda's terrorism wanted to destroy.

The Istanbul attacks confronted the AKP government with a test. A test of strength, first of all, that has turned to the advantage of the government, which was able to dismantle the Islamist networks and arrest their members. But also an intellectual and political test for the party's leaders, who have been forced, under pressure from secular intellectuals and democrats, to recognize the religious nature of terrorism. They also had to clearly demonstrate their determination not to accept the interpretation of Islam that terrorism wants to impose and thus destroy an important aspect of the Ottoman heritage in modern Turkey, namely the presence of Judaism.. The visit made by the prime minister, Tayyip Erdoğan, to the Chief Rabbi of Turkey is of primordial importance, because it is not only a governmental expression of solidarity with the Jewish community of Istanbul, but also a gesture of public recognition of Judaism as a religion and its right to exist in Turkey. Paradoxically, a secular politician might have been less sensitive to the religion of the Jewish minority in Turkey.

If Turkey was chosen as a local site for Islamist global terrorism, that is because it might constitute a model for moving beyond the clash of civilizations and a point of transition between Islam and the Western world. The targets chosen, banks and synagogues, stage on the global scale a repertory of Islamist radicalism that seeks to challenge the legitimacy of financial capitalism and the practice of Judaism in the land of Islam. We can see in this how anti-Semitism and anti-Judaism are becoming signs of the confrontation between radical Islamism and the Western world but also and especially between different interpretations of Islam. Paradoxically, and this is perplexing, it seems that Al-Qaeda was able to locate, in order to try to destroy them, Muslim modernity and Muslim Europeanness even before they were recognized and supported by the European powers.

During the following decade, the question of anti-Semitism and foreign policy with regard to Israel became more and more decisive in detecting and interpreting the orientation of the AKP government toward the Western world on the one hand and toward the Islamic world on the other. Whether Turkey is becoming a central interlocutor between the two or turning away from its Western European attachments is now a central question. Turkish foreign policy is gaining a new orientation and impetus, leaving the cold-war status quo behind. The National Assembly's rejection in March 2003 of a motion to permit the United States to use bases in Turkey for launching attacks on Iraq constituted a turning point in the process of autonomization of Turkish foreign politics from the grip of the United States. Turkey gained respect in the eyes of the Middle East countries and among reformist Muslims, in imposing itself, by means of a democratically elected popular government, as a major actor in the region standing against the United States. A series of events brought Turkey and its prime minister, albeit unintentionally to the forefront of the global stage. During the World Economic Forum's meeting in Davos (January 2009), Prime Minister Recep Tayyip Erdogan and Israeli President Shimon Peres debated fiercely the Israel's Gaza offensive. Erdogan protested not having the possibility to respond and asked for "a minute." Disappointed, he left the panel, and the diplomatic incident was named thereafter as the "one minute" protest.[10] Turkish Israeli relations continued to deteriorate with the failed attempt of Turkey to make a new deal alongside Brazil on Iran's nuclear program. The relations between the two countries came to a critical momentum with the "Flotilla crisis" in May 2010. Against the Gaza blockade imposed by the Israeli government after the Islamist movement Hamas took power in 2007, the Free Gaza movement, an international coalition aiming to break the three-year Israeli closure was organized with the active participation of Turkish Muslim humanitarian aid organization. The six-ship flotilla, carrying humanitarian aid and heading toward Gaza was stopped in international waters by the intervention of Israeli commandos, causing casualties and killing nine activists, mostly of Turkish citizenship. The Turkish prime minister accused Israel of state terrorism, while the Israeli government criticized the campaign as a "provocation," intending to delegitimize the Israeli state.

For some observers, Turkey, being rejected by Europe, tries to gain popularity in the Arab street and join instead the "Arab league." Turkey is feared to be turning its back against Western values and taking a hard line against Israel, not only that it adopts a populist rhetoric and allows the rise of anti-Semitic feelings among the population but also that it gives up the promise to be a mediator and becomes instead an ally of the nondemocratic elements in the East, including Iran.[11] For other observers, on the contrary, in holding the Palestinian card, Turkey is positioned as the central interlocutor between the Islamic/Arab world and Israel, relegating Iran to a marginal influence.[12] In this perspective even if Turkey ceases to align her interests with that of the West, it can become the standard-bearer of the Islamic world. One more big step is required for Turkey to enter the history, namely calling the Islamists and Iran to recognize the Israeli state.[13]

Whether Turkey is a new emerging global actor transmitting values of liberalism and pluralism, or on the contrary a "torn-between country" witnessing the incompatibility and confrontation between two sets of values and civilizations continues to be an open-end question.

CHAPTER 5

Islam and Globalization: Similarity or Alterity?

Globalization entails new connections between markets, governments, and cultures.[1] Technologies of communication shape and strengthen these new types of interconnections in a way that is more transnational than national: with them, a shift is taking place from the social organization supervised by the autonomous nation-state and attached to a territory, to a transversal and virtual "connectivity" on the global scale. The public space, markets, universities, and social movements are no longer limited to a national space and a territory but are linked by the circulation of products, information, people, and ideas. This transversality means a greater synchronization of social practices but not their homogenization.

Interpretations of globalization, like those of protest movements, tend to be made from the point of view of the central countries.[2] They are implicitly based on a definition of the center, and consequently on a division between sites where the power of financial capitalism is concentrated (notably the United States) and those that undergo its consequences. Globalization from above, which has control over financial capitalism, and globalization from below, the anti-globalization movements that protest it, depend on a vertical conception of these phenomena. Moreover, this conception assumes that the groups on the margins of the system, the ones that are subject to it, are the most capable of developing feelings and strategies of opposition. However, for many of them, globalization means an opportunity for "opening up" and inclusion: many young consumers, activists, and entrepreneurs see satellite TV channels, humanitarian organizations, ecology movements, and international financial institutions (like the IMF and the World Bank) as sources of exchange and participation. The reforms the IMF imposed on Argentina and Turkey are supported by a nonnegligible part of public opinion that aspires to be included in the global economy and finds it risky and expensive to remain outside the system. Furthermore, organizations such as Amnesty International, Greenpeace, and Human Rights Watch offer an opportunity for critical international action and constitute a worldwide space of membership and exchange with other activists, professionals, and humanitarians, including those of the central countries. By the content of their action, but also and especially as physical spaces, these organizations are becoming vehicles for implementing transversal "connectivities." They provide opportunities for integration into global networks of discursive practices and political vigilance, which in turn provide, in the national framework, public power and recognition for those who belong to these militant networks. The more peripheral the country, the more access to global networks provides local power. A decentered approach to globalization and to criticisms of it has to take into account these asymmetries between those who are near the centers of development and those who are far away from them.

A question of taxonomy arises: what are the criteria, and who establishes them, that enable us to consider one practice global and another local?[3] To call a practice "local" means that it has no general, universal scope, that it is anchored in an unconscious geographical space, in a culturally given era, and thus that it is limited. However, modernity leads to a process of deracination with respect to places, traditions, and religions. Modernity and mobility are intrinsically connected insofar as the movement of modernity means being torn away from roots and primordial memberships.[4] It is because a population is uprooted, displaced, that it is defined as modern, universal, and cosmopolitan. Only those who have this capacity for mobility and distancing (the intellectual, the businessman) enter into the era of modernity. The idea of deterritorialization and circulation is present at the dawn of modernity; it differentiates those who are not mobile and attached to a specific place. The narrative of modernity thus does not accord local practices a general and universal import. Today, approaches to globalization seem to be giving new importance to the local, but they do so only to reproduce the same hierarchized taxonomy that distinguishes between the universal and mobile center and the local, the particularist, and the limited. The relation the West maintains with the Other, the relationship to difference, thus remains extremely problematic, both for the instigators of globalization and for its critics. That is why a decentered approach to globalization can bring out new problems of taxonomy and forces us to rethink power relationships and modes of knowledge.

Another normative aspect is involved in the taxonomies of the anti-globalization movement. Only the critical and progressive movements that have emerged from the social movements of the 1970s or in their wake, such as the ecology movement, associations against racism, the peasant movement, and feminism, are supposed to be worthy of being classified and studied as anti-globalization movements. Nationalist, extreme right-wing groups in Europe are not easily included in this list. and Islamist movements still less. Until the September 11 attacks, Islam did not figure in the literature on globalization. Since then, Islam has not only emerged in this literature but occupies a central place in it. How can we approach the complex relationship between Islam and globalization? On the one hand, Islam acts in a globalized world; on the other hand, it is becoming a factor of globalization, while at the same time bringing out the relationship to alterity in a world that is both more integrated and more divided.

With globalization, a transnational dimension of the public sphere is beginning to put its stamp on political life. As an autonomous gathering place in relation to the state and a space for debate, the public sphere definitively constituted itself in Europe in the course of the eighteenth century. It defined a model (an ideal type, in Jürgen Habermas's approach[5]) of autonomy and openness such that every citizen has free access to it and can publicly debate the city's affairs. There is a connection between democracy and the public sphere as it is conceived in this European model, a connection that Axel Honneth explains when he adds that the public sphere constitutes a place of social struggles, and thus of active conflictuality, and not a single, unified, homogeneous space.[6] But today the boundaries of the public space have been displaced—by its transnational dimensions, on the one hand, and by its virtual dimensions on the other. This can strengthen or renew "connectivities" within the diversity of cultures. But above all it poses the question of transnational public spaces and their connection with politics: to what extent do these spaces allow relationships of domination, stigmatization, and exclusion to be translated into political consciousness and put on the public agenda?

In any event, Islam has been propelled to the front of the world stage since the terrorist acts of September 11, 2001. It has made its appearance in the American public space, which up to that time had been relatively indifferent to the Islamic phenomenon. Thus we could see President George W. Bush in a mosque, or discover that CNN and Al-Jazeera had exchanged information and engaged in joint interpretations in translating articles published in other national spaces. The connections between the different media were strengthened, new modes of exchange were launched. The Turkish daily newspaper *Radikal* published Western and Muslim opinion pieces; the Paris daily *Le Monde* offered a weekly supplement taken from the *New York Times*. In addition, the interest aroused by the phenomenon of Islam (including the Qur'an) increased, and experts on or spokesmen for Islam, who had long been confined to the cultural sphere or to orientalism, came to occupy a more central space in the social sciences. Transnational research on Islam has replaced approaches limited to the national level. Not only can a commentator write that "Islam is globalized,"[7] but whereas before Islam was not part of the literature on globalization, it has now become an active agent in the circulation of ideas, products, and persons, and is consequently contributing to the emergence of a transnational public space.

Globalness and Islam

The September 11 terrorist attacks can serve as a guide for analyzing the change in direction taken by the relationship between Islam and globalness.

These attacks took place in a global public space. Perhaps for the first time in history, a terrorist event was witnessed live as a visual and media experience by a very large number of people. The events were apprehended individually, simultaneously, and on a global scale. But they were understood differently depending on the different public spaces to which those who were witnessing them belonged. September 11 deepened gaps while at the same time reaching various publics and strengthening the relations between them. Indeed, both America and Afghanistan, brought together by the image, were newcomers to globalization. Americans "have tragically rejoined the rest of the world," Dick Howard wrote,[8] and *The New York Times* could describe New York as it might any city of the third world, that is, as chaotic and in ruins.[9] The shock also proceeded from the discovery of the vulnerability of American power. For its part, Afghanistan, which up to that point had been abandoned to the Taliban's anti-modernist movement, made its entry on the scene of modern history thanks to Ben Laden's terrorist engineering. September 11 illustrates the process of globalization as a reduction of distances, a juxtaposition of histories and cultures. A process that in turn initiated not reconciliation between different parts of the world but on the contrary, their mutual apprehension, and even their clash. It is possible to advance the hypothesis that the cleavages grow deeper and are felt more intensely as proximity increases, and that the stake involved is the dividing up of space.

September 11 became a turning point in relations between globalization and Islam, on the one hand because it emphasized a clash of civilizations (Samuel Huntington's thesis gained ground) and on the other hand because it elicited a critique of American policy (as is shown by several recent studies of anti-Americanism). In other words, while globalization is more and more often identified with the Americanization of capitalism and ways of life, Islamization is considered a global civilizational threat. The perception of the conflict in terms of civilization follows the dynamics of globalization and at the same time sees American policy as both the cause and the remedy at the heart of historical action.

The question of action and responsibility deserves examination. Among the arguments seeking to explain the causes of the conflict, and more precisely the "hatred," many writers have insisted on inequalities and social injustice. From this point of view, it is not a matter of religion, but of impoverished and deprived groups that nourish a feeling of injustice. Don't such sharp differences create a destabilizing gap that can arouse a thirst for vengeance among the victims? This kind of analysis is often accompanied by a criticism of financial capitalism and American policy. However we have already seen how the thought, often prominent on the left, that looks into the role of the West in the course of events can itself mask a certain arrogance by attributing to the West complete responsibility for what has taken place. For their part, Muslim publics escape their responsibility by seeing themselves as dominated and victimized or by finding conspiracy theories that attack the "Jewish lobbies," although the September 11 attacks tried, even if only during the terrorist action itself, to reverse the roles and to transform the Americans into victims.

The terrorist actors can also be described as having emerged from globalization. Most of them are transnationals and do not live in their countries of origin; they have often studied abroad, speak Western languages, and travel from one country to another.[10] They consider themselves Muslims but not citizens of a specific country. They are deracinated and deterritorialized. Their religiousness is defined more by an individualist conception than by membership in a community or a territory. Terrorism emerges, as Michel Wieviorka has observed,[11] from the context of the national question and, more clearly, from geopolitics; it testifies to a territorial detachment, and is becoming global.

The choice of targets on September 11, 2001, the Pentagon and the World Trade Center, reflects not only anti-Americanism but also a logic of anti-globalization.

Terrorism can be seen as an omen and an exacerbation of this ongoing destabilization of the hegemonic relationship of the West to the Muslim world. Increased proximity, supported by the logic of the media on a global scale, makes every part of the world a potential site (a train station in Madrid, a discotheque in Bali, a theater in Moscow, skyscrapers in New York) of terrorist activity.[12] Globalization and terrorism are indeed connected.

The amalgam of terrorist acts and ecological catastrophe underlies conflicts on the global scale. Terrorism seems to take on the character of an environmental disaster by provoking war. But within the cases of both the declaration of a jihad and the "war on terrorism," it is difficult to define the boundaries and the duration of the hostilities. Conflicts circulate and acquire the appearance of catastrophes. Thus Craig Calhoun has shown how the same term, *emergency,* is used to describe both conflicts and natural catastrophes or human suffering worldwide. According to him, this term naturalizes and dissimulates conflicts by erasing their political and diachronic dimension (as if they were sudden and punctual events like emergencies), while at the same time appealing for humanitarian aid from world organizations.[13]

What are the major conflicts that underlie globalization? How can we understand and name the new forms of domination, exclusion, and inequalities established during this phase of history? The notion of conflict, which is central to the epoch of industrial (class conflict) and national modernity, is being corroded. A slippage toward a logic of confrontation that amalgamates terrorism, war, catastrophe, and ethnic cleansing testifies to the transformation of the scale of conflicts at the same time that it dissimulates them. Globalization imposes itself, as Alain Touraine observes, in the form of a normative ideology dissimulating power relationships, exclusions, and dominations.[14] It operates like a market: without a face, without an actor, without subjectivity. Terrorism erupts in a way that inverts globalization and at the same time imitates it: without identity, without a face (or veiled, as in the case of the Chechen female terrorists), without a voice, as an act of pure destruction.

It is also symptomatic of the absence of political space on the global level. While the relationship to the Other defines the boundaries of the political, globalization, by its transversality, seeks to move beyond national, cultural, and religious differences. The relationship to difference has become more problematic in the global era of modernity. Perhaps the problem is not to discover how to take difference into account, to recognize it and contain it (that is, the debate on multiculturalism), but rather to discover how to maintain the boundaries of difference, to define a subjectivity, to construct an alterity.

Similitude and proximity

Globalization forces us to apprehend the relation between Islam and modernity in terms of proximity, and not of cultural and geographical distance, as do analyses that talk about the clash of civilizations.

Monotheism, and especially colonialism, deliberate modernization, and today globalization and immigration have led Muslim groups to experiment with modernity. The latter is becoming a reality more endogenous than exogenous, more indigenous than imposed from above or by the West. The indigenization of modernity also signifies a more lateral and personal relation to modernity. Globalization leads to a certain distancing of modernity from the Western model as other cultures appropriate it, contextualize it, and even turn it away from its origins. This appropriation, as was moreover already the case during colonial expansion, is not achieved smoothly, without conflicts and without suffering, in the course of an evolutionary development. On the contrary, it takes place by exacerbating questions relating to self-definition in modernity. Contemporary Islamism is symptomatic of this conflictual indigenization. Islam is coming back in force at a moment in history when Muslim populations have grown accustomed to modern experience.

Such a proximity creates new sources of tension and conflict. Islam thus dramatically incarnates the fear of similitude. In the modern world, which is governed by the implementation of resemblances, religious and cultural certainties based on "natural" boundaries are shaken. Woman is, symbolically and corporeally, the pivot of these transformations. We have also seen how the interchangeability of roles, clothing, and even genders, is rendered commonplace by modernity, which makes any difference a source of hybridization and crossbreeding. But the modern world never ceases to gain ground, even in the Muslim world. Against a lack of differentiation, the exacerbated reference to Islam aims to maintain, or more precisely, to recreate, boundaries between the private and the public, between men and women, between the Muslim world and the Western world. In a world in which nothing can resist the rapidity of change, the emphasis put on the ephemeral, on pleasure, on cultural experience, where everything follows the groove of a secular logic, including the body and reproduction, it is through religion that the limits of the forbidden are recalled.

This does not mean, however, that Islamism and Islam are one and the same thing. Although in its acts it refers to the religious repertory, Islamism is far from being faithful to the religious tradition. Its discourse is simplistic, anachronistic, and lacks solid references to the

Qur'an. It proceeds by amalgamation, realizing a kind of syncretism of various traditions, cultures, or religious schools. Thus the return to Islam that it advocates is related to a misappropriation of religious traditions and the authority connected with the interpretation of the text of the Qur'an is subjected to a democratic erosion.

The actors of Islamism, shaped far less by religion than by modernity, present for the time being a hybrid character, crossbred and impure, like the neomartyrs, Islamist engineers, and female legislators sitting in the Turkish parliament wearing the Islamic headscarf.[15] They are not defined and limited by any religious or community membership. The martyrs are not defending a territory, the engineers have received a secular, rational education, and the veiled women are leaving the enclosed space of the private and demanding access to university campuses and to membership in parliament. The actors of Islam are gaining a public visibility. They are in a logic of mobility with regard to their original milieu; they no longer represent the "local Muslim," either by their membership in a group or by the meaning of their action. They are putting into practice and circulation a new collective Muslim imagination. The globalized object is this new collective imaginary.

The Muslim collective imagination

This concept of a collective imagination is what best accounts for Islam today. Unlike Islamist ideology, which is rigid and whose interpretation and circulation are limited to intellectuals and activists, the collective imagination is addressed to a broader population and is based on the idea of a cultural repertory.[16] This imagination develops with reference to Islamism but with a more general scope, because it cannot be limited to a political commitment and a discursive practice. The Islamic imagination circulates at the global level without taking into account national boundaries or religious differences. What is "globalized" is this imagination in circulation. On the other hand, Islamism takes very different forms depending on the political contexts: revolution and terrorism but also a commitment to parliamentary government, as the Turkish case has recently shown. These cases put in question again even the term *Islamism*.

It was, we must repeat, the September 11 attacks that unveiled this new imagination that had up to that time taken form in silence, independently of national or religious differences. Terrorism attacks political icons, or rather "metapolitical" icons,[17] to which it gives a religious resonance that is clearly visible in Islam. This does not mean that Muslim peoples approve of terrorist acts. But in any case these acts become unavoidable points of reference in relation to which Muslims feel forced to define themselves or to distance themselves. The Islamic imagination is not put into circulation solely by terrorist acts but also and especially by everyday practices. Public debates about the Islamic veil in the schools, the construction of mosques, halal meat, the Western calendar, and the status of the imam thus illustrate the diversity of the micro-actions in countries with Muslim majorities, as well as in those with large Muslim immigrant populations. It is not the imposition of Sharia by seizing state power that defines the Islamist movement but rather these "performative" and oppositional practices that seek to create a place for religion in the public space. As the notion of "imagination" suggests, action is transmitted by images, icons; a more "performative" politics closer to the senses and especially to the visual is at work. The Islamic imagination is transmitted by the repetition of these practices, which are anchored in everyday life and draw sustenance from a cultural and religious model, seeking to distinguish themselves from modernity's definition of the liberal subject.[18]

Islamism causes the emergence of a politics that is closer to the body and to space, a politics that is more visual and thus more media-oriented on the global public stage.

CHAPTER 6

Modernity, Taxonomies: Global and Local

It might be more accurate to speak of "local modernities," because the reference to the local dimension of modernity already assumes a shift from a monist conception of modernity to a pluralist one. The deconstruction of the modernist project of assimilation, of the system of the same, of the total vision of the Western tradition, now guides critical thought in the human sciences. Once the exclusive equation of the West with modernity has been broken, we can see the multiplicity of local, historical, and cultural forms that modernity can take. Attention to "local modernity" thus precedes the critique undertaken by theories of postcolonialism and orientalism. But while the latter stresses the conception and construction of the Other by the West, an approach in terms of "local modernity" implies a reversal of the perspective, giving priority to the interpretation of modernity through the prism of the historical practice of non-Western countries. Turning toward local modernities thus implies both a theoretical and an intellectual decentering with respect to the West.

In fact, the swing of the pendulum from a universalist to a particularist conception of modernity is accompanied by the emergence of a new intellectual sensibility. Intellectuals, artists, and writers of a new kind share the desire to draw from the past neglected cultural references and to win back memory in order to understand and invent hybrid forms intermediate between subjectivity and modernity. As Abdelwahab Meddeb has put it,[1] it is a matter of turning back on oneself for the "critical transformation" of non-Western countries.

This presupposes going to seek out, rummage through, and bring to light the "untranslatable," something that resists the language of the social sciences,[2] the grip of modernity. In other words, we have to turn our eyes toward what is specific, what is singular in endogenous practices, instead of ignoring them because they are not compatible with the logic of Western modernity. It is sometimes in these practices, in these notes, these words considered as pathological, outdated, reactionary, or kitsch that the key to social innovation and intellectual understanding lies. Of course, what non-Western societies allow us to hear is not clear, their music is not composed, their historical practice and their knowledge are not in harmony. But this "cacophony" is an additional reason to try to listen, to attend to what is atypical and unprecedented in order to make it intelligible through scientific, literary, or artistic language.

Thus we must substitute distrust for our confidence in concepts and, as Gilles Deleuze urges philosophers to do, work out, invent, or create concepts in an incessant confrontation with the world, history, and social practice.[3] Such an effort to know oneself, to act as if nothing could be taken for granted, and thus to be astonished and look at everything with new eyes, requires critical conceptual labor. Only this critical force of the concept[4] will make it possible to avoid, by breaking the bonds of dominant Western thinking, the annihilation of the self through reduction to the Same or, on the contrary, by reduction to an Other thought to be of a different essence. Although the first intellectual position has been criticized for asserting the primacy of the Same, of the West, and thus reducing to silence the Other, the peoples dominated by assimilation, the second position, much favored these days, hardly avoids reducing the Other to silence by recognizing it as exotic and external. The two attitudes amount to the same insofar as they fail to recognize that the production of knowledge is a matter of interhuman, intersubjective communication. They do not situate the non-West as an interlocutor, as a subject anchored in a dialogic relationship, as a source of knowledge about the West. Rethinking modernity from two points of view, connected histories between Western and non-Western, is no easy task. Reversing the perspective and shifting the focus to non-Western modernity, we must undertake reconstituting the dialectical connection between identity and alterity and not break it in a new way.

Rethinking modernity by establishing a dialogue between the non-West and the histories, social practices, and subjectivity of the West is no easy task. Such an intersection of views on the respective practices requires special vigilance to discern in the concepts and taxonomies the relations of domination, dependency, and denigration. This is not a matter of reciprocity; on the contrary, as Talal Asad has written, the opposition (and hence the link) between the West and the non-West is based on an asymmetry of desires and forms of indifference.[5] The history of non-Western countries cannot be written independently of that of Western modernity. The historical and intellectual trajectory of these countries is traversed by the awareness of a backwardness with respect to the West and a desire for modernity. Constant comparison with the West disturbs, indeed distorts, the action and analysis of non-Western actors. Rather ironically, social actors feel themselves to be "outside" their own history and praxis. Insofar as they do not feel themselves to be the masters of their own actions and analyses, the desire to violently cut the bond of dependency on the West (reversal through third-worldism or Islamism) and to overcome their alienation by recourse to conspiracy theories characterizes the action and the mentalities of non-Western countries. In other words, we find the mark of this problematic relation to the West both in their political history, their praxis, and in their intellectual personalities.

Thus we cannot study the history of Muslim countries and the trajectories of Muslim lives without taking into account the bond of dependency. However, this dependency, which infiltrates collective history, action, and consciousness, is manifested in an endogenous way. In other words, on the local level there exist many specific ways of appropriating Western modernity. The latter appears as an abstract, selective construction that changes in relation to the geographical or historical space and also over time. Thus the modernist elites of the late nineteenth century saw the Occidental experiment as a model of "civilization" and "progress," whereas for third-world intellectuals of the 1970s, the West appeared to be responsible for "exploitation" and "underdevelopment." Or again, during the 1980s, while liberals maintained that everyone had to participate in global modernity, the Islamists, for their part, thought they had to rediscover their "authenticity" and reject the model of the state, society, and the individual that had been shaped by Western modernity.

From intellectual imitation to the indigenous intellectual

It is this endogenous character of modernity in non-Western countries that is designated by the term *local modernity*. It presupposes that modernity is not external to the history, the imagination, and the social practice of these countries. It set out to study the exacerbated, perverted, distorted forms, or, to put it very simply, the ways in which modernity is appropriated in a non-Western context. The concept of local also has its limits because it falls into the trap we seek to avoid by leading us to suppose that local practice is "authentic," "pure," or "uncontaminated by modernity"—that it is different in essence.

The new sensitivity in Western social sciences that seeks to "give a voice to the oppressed" can lead, as we have already seen, to an inverted way of perpetuating relations of domination in the area of the production of knowledge.[6] Interest in particularism and ethnic identity is accompanied, for the Other, by a near refusal of access to the universal, to modernity, to knowledge. The Other has a right to exist only insofar as he does not cross boundaries, insofar as he remains local, autochthonous. Although non-Western intellectuals are recognized by the universalist approach so long as they transmit progressive Western values, that is, so long as they are agents of the West's civilizing mission, they play the role of translators, inverting the flow and transmitting ideas from the local to the West. In the universalist mode of thought, the intellectual emerges in the context of a modernist elite, defines himself by his membership in "high culture," and finds his particularist legitimacy in his resemblance to the "civilized" person, the Westerner. In the particularist mode, on the contrary, the more he adopts the local color of authenticity, the closer he is to "popular culture," or better yet, to the "excluded," the more he is recognized. It is preferable that his physical appearance and his social, ethnic, or religious background allow him to make the claim to be different, authentic, and present himself as a spokesperson for that identity-related difference. A new kind of intellectual, the imitator, finds it possible to address a Western audience by impoverishing the hybrid character of social reality and essentializing the differences. Here we can suggest that when ideas are transmitted from the local to the global, what is "good for the Orient" gradually gives way to what is "good for the West." The "indigenous" intellectual, once deprived (having intentionally deprived himself or herself) of conceptual and critical power, remains imprisoned in the Western imagination and gives up all intellectual creativity and originality, complacently adopting the role of Lawrence of Arabia in reverse. As contradictory as it may seem, the indigenous intellectual also finds an echo in the local context, insofar as he rejects assimilation to the West and strengthens ideologies related to ethnic identity.

Thus taxonomies in terms of the local, endogenous, or particularist do not escape the grip of power relationships between the West and other countries in the domain of knowledge. Furthermore, by virtue of what criterion can one distinguish certain actions or expressions considered as local from others that are allegedly universal, if not by their failure to reproduce the West's spatial and cultural hierarchy? To describe a reality, a culture, or a people as "local" implies that they are attached to a territory, rooted, and thus limited in their world and their action, unlike those who are mobile, cosmopolitan, and universal.[7] Since a positive relation is established between mobility and modernity, the term *local* can signify a lack of mobility, of change, of invention. Consequently, the indigenization of the intellectual is almost a contradiction in terms, and renouncing the "mobile personality" (to use Daniel Lerner's expression,[8] amounts to renouncing the transformative and creative capacity of the modern condition. It is by their capacity for movement, for putting themselves in the place of the Other through empathy, that intellectuals can renew their way of confronting the world.[9]

It is only by resituating themselves at the intersection of their own local history with modernity, by sketching their asymmetrical trajectories, and by recognizing their own hybrid character, that non-Western intellectuals will be able to carry out a critical transformation of knowledge and thus clear the way for overcoming the dependency, the "weak historicity" (Alain Touraine) of their societies, that is, their lesser capacity to produce their own history and culture. A decentering with respect to the West and a distancing with respect to local practice are both prerequisites for the creation of a new critical space of reflection. Original conceptual power can proceed only from this double tension, from this synergy of modernity and local experience.

Intellectual decentering with respect to the West leads us to take into account the experiences of non-Western countries and to establish between them horizontal relationships of contrast, comparison, and understanding. Universalist and monist modernity has set up hierarchized, vertical relations between non-Western countries and the West, to the detriment of horizontal, neighborhood relations. Each of these countries has positioned and measured itself by reference to the Western model, without seeing itself, without reading itself, in the historical and cultural mirror of other non-Western countries. Thus the mental distance separating them seems to be greater than the geographical and cultural proximity. On the other hand, the approach in terms of local modernity, by constructing the object of study as a mode of appropriation specific to modernity, privileges horizontal relationships.[10] The question is whether something common and peculiar to local modernity can justify the use of such a term in the singular, allowing us to avoid falling into the absolute relativism of postmodernism. Otherwise we would be left with a multiplicity of local forms characterizing our inability to engender and name the experience of these countries. They would still remain societies "without a name," a residue of the "West" called the "non-West"; they would be confined within geographical or religious boundaries, etc.

Detraditionalization and the past

In non-Western contexts, we can speak of a particular discord between tradition and modernity that has been introduced either by voluntary, programmed modernization or by the experience of being colonized. Although they are often described as "traditional," these societies have been traversed by a detraditionalization, a rejection of the past. In some countries where it is especially the authoritarian forms of modernization that have prevailed, the break with the past, with traditions, is still more radical. Turkey, among Muslim nations, but also China, can be given as examples of programmed detraditionalization.[11] The radical rejection of the past became the motivating ideology of the modernist revolution of Kemalism, as well as of Maoist communism, even though they are very different from one another.[12]

But it is not the celebration of modernity, of novelty as opposed to traditions, that characterizes non-Western modernization. This opposition is itself a characteristic of Western modernity.[13] Instead, non-Western modernization is characterized by the noncontinuity, or even the noncorrespondence between traditions and modern practices, which appear as dissonant components. In other terms, neither modernization nor secularization emerges from a critical study of religious traditions; the latter are consequently rejected, repressed, or forgotten and left to themselves. Fragments of modern life coexist with traditions, without any exchange taking place between them.

Urban space bears witness to this dissonant and fragmented nature of local modernity, which is also characterized by a lack of temporal continuity. What Ackbar Abbas says about Hong Kong could be said of Istanbul as well: it is a space traversed by different times and tempos, where change does not occur in a clear direction, with a weakening of the sense of chronology, of historical continuity, that leads to the contemporary coexistence of the new and the old, the premodern connecting with the postmodern without either being forced to recognize the other.[14] The discontinuity between traditional Turkish cafes and Western-style cafes, which are becoming more and more fashionable in Istanbul, is an example of this. Traditional coffee houses are frequented by men from the neighborhood; they play cards, watch a game on television, discuss politics; these neighborhood cafes, which are almost invisible to the modern Turkish eye, succeed in surviving here and there in Istanbul, within the local limits of community life. On the other hand, the fashionable cafes that have opened in large numbers everywhere in Istanbul over the past few years are places where both men and women gather; one can have lunch in them at noon, but in the afternoon they become bars, and in the late evening they serve as discotheques. It is hard to speak of a continuity between these two types of cafes. Not only is the famous Turkish coffee being replaced on menus by the popular espresso and cappuccino, but even in ordinary language the word *cafe* is written and pronounced as in English.

The use of private spaces does not escape an aesthetics fragmented into the fetish objects of modernity and traditional habits. The dining table and the buffet are both signs of conspicuous consumption, even in modest social classes; however, in everyday life, we still find many households where the dining table is reserved for guests, while the family prefers to sit around a low round table and eat its meals sitting on the floor.

Paradoxically, contemporary Islamism also participates in this process of detraditionalization and at the same time in the desire to return to tradition. The Islamic veil for women is the most visible symbol of this ethnic questioning of both modernity and traditions.

The reappearance of the veil is surprising and disturbing, because it goes back to religious traditions that were supposed to have disappeared under the impact of modernization. It is interpreted by public opinion in both Western and Muslim countries as a sign of the failure of modernization projects. The veil is all the more disturbing because it has emerged in spaces of modernity such as large cities and university campuses. The terminology chosen to refer to the contemporary Islamic article of clothing reveals the unprecedented character of the phenomenon. The use of the word *veil* is not pertinent if it is taken to refer only to the practice of covering the face.[15] In the European media, there is a continual semantic shift in the use of the terms used to designate Islamic covering: *headscarf, hijab, nikap,* and now *burka,* the latter referring to the total covering of women's bodies. Although the burka is worn by very few women and criticized by all sides, including Muslims, in France it has become a legal issue and provoked a general debate on French "national identity." Women wearing the burka, retreating from the public sphere and hiding their faces, have become a subject of fear for European democracies that cherish visibility and transparence. But wearing some such covering is far from being a distinctive sign in Muslim countries, because many women in both the countryside and the large cities wear a traditional shawl over their heads without that having political or religious significance. To mark the difference with the traditional headscarf, the Turkish press has identified the new phenomenon as a movement of women in "turbans." This description seeks to indicate women's active appropriation and the affirmation of a collective identity in contrast to passive transmission from one generation to another. This term *turban* says a great deal about the ambivalence and transgressions in Islamist women's behavior as well as in the representations attributed to them. The word *turban* comes from *tülbend*, in Turkish, or from *dülband*, in Persian, terms that designate the light linen, cotton, or silk fabric that covers the head. However, today the Western word *turban* is used to describe a new way of covering one's hair and head. In this sense, *turban* has undergone a change in meaning, and is located on the dividing line between Eastern and Western meanings and practices. It refers to a fashion, and clearly indicates change, the modern way of appropriating the act of covering one's head in contrast to traditions that perpetuate themselves. On the other hand, the turban is also a masculine headdress made of a long strip of cloth rolled about the head, and often worn by the pious. Using this term instead of the feminine *headscarf,* acknowledges a "power" that Muslim women have, indicates their "virilization" by religious politics, whatever their intentions might be. If the fact of wearing a veil evokes traditional definitions of feminine identity based on the enclosure of women and segregation of the sexes, these Islamist women, having access to politics and education, are leaving the closed space of the private world and thus moving beyond the traditional roles that have been assigned to them. In other words, the very term *turban* conceals and reveals the hybrid, transgressive character of the Islamic veil, which finds itself at the intersection of the dynamics of power relationships between East and West, tradition and modernity, men and women.

Furthermore, unlike the traditional veil—which varies from one region to another, both in its color and in the way it is worn—contemporary Islamic dress for women is more or less uniform, and seems rather transregional or transnational, thus designating a common political consciousness and a collective attitude. The fabric, color, and cut are inspired by modern fashion trends. Its shape reflects more the silhouette of the Western woman, muscular and triangular, with accentuated shoulders, than the oriental silhouette of fluid femininity in the form of a "bell" (as in the case of women wearing the *chador*).

At the very moment that we thought the process of detraditionalization was coming to a conclusion and that global modernity was going to win out over local ways of life and identities, we are witnessing a renewal of interest in the memory of the past that draws on rejected cultural signs, takes its inspiration from autochthonous aesthetics, and revives forgotten traditions. However this is neither a matter of returning to traditions nor of some kind of desire to go back to the golden age, but rather of a difficult attempt to reconstruct the connection between subjectivity and modernity, whose rupture is the characteristic trait of non-Western modernity.

CHAPTER 7

Extra-Modernities

Working on modes of configuring Islam in contemporary Muslim societies, and in particular in Turkish society, I am pursuing my research at the École des hautes études en sciences sociales in Paris in connection with the "Center for sociological analysis and action" and also with a center for cultural area studies, the "Center for the history of the Turkish area." From the point of view of the object I study, contemporary Islam, this intersection between sociology, which gives priority to the present time, and cultural area studies, which take historical, cultural, and religious specificity into account, is entirely desirable and appropriate. But in reality, there are very few links between the two domains.

All research on an area like Turkey—which, while being an extra-European country, is exemplary in its historical desire to be open to Western modernity—naturally leads to the question of the connection between the narrative of modernity and cultural specificity. European modernity and its social imagination are disseminated, infiltrating and circulating in extra-European spaces, through deliberate, programmed modernization, as in Turkey, following colonialism, as in India, or with globalization. Thus we can speak, with regard to these diverse contexts, of an indigenization of modernity whose adoption does not take place without collisions and subversions. But as we have already seen, this process acts in return to transform the definitions of modernity. Our time suggests a new reading of modernity, on its margins, through the forms that it takes in non-Western spaces. However, this reading cannot be taken for granted; it implies a critical perspective on the monist narrative of modernity as well as on certain conceptual distortions that obscure the theoretical fecundity of non-European practices.

Locality and mobility

Sociological theory, which provides chiefly a Eurocentric interpretation of modernity based on the assumption of a universalist and evolutionary history, reveals its limits when it is a question of interpreting and explaining the selective and specialized ways in which modernity is appropriated in non-European spaces. The approach by cultural areas fails to problematize the relationship to modernity; reflection is limited to a single space, confined, as it were, to an enclave, and thus only increases the gap between knowledge that is supposed to be universal in scope and particular knowledge contained within narrow boundaries. Describing a people and its social practices as "local" implies that they are attached to a place and a limited range, by contrast to mobile, cosmopolitan, and universal practices.[1] The renewal of interest in the study of practices on the "local" level thus contributes to our understanding of the singularity of phenomena but not to changing our interpretation of modernity; on the contrary.

However, as Talal Asad points out, global and local taxonomies must be conceived of in connection with relationships of power and knowledge.[2] In fact, today it is difficult to deal with religious phenomena as local, that is, as bound to a space, a locality. Contemporary Islam is a perfect illustration of this. Islamist actors are more often characterized by their mobility than by their geographical, national, or religious ties. This mobility has often been described in negative terms, as a dispossession and alienation of actors who are déclassé and participate in the rural exodus and deterritorialization. But that is to forget that modernity and mobilization are related in a particular and positive way. Any process of detachment from a place, a tradition, or a specific community has as its consequence a strengthening of the personal dimension of convictions and action. Islam has in fact become a reference point for individuals who are distancing themselves from their origins and crossing geographical and cultural borders in search of new opportunities for education and life. Islam is no longer transmitted from one generation to the next; it no longer appears as a norm imposed by the community to which one belongs but is being, on the contrary, "reinvented." The bond that it constitutes no longer proceeds exclusively from connection with a local, religious, and national group but becomes "imaginary" for those who are socially deracinated and are seeking to reconstruct horizontal connections. The term *Islamist* refers to this phenomenon. Deracination, or social mobility, becomes a precondition for the shift from Islam to Islamism, for the transformation of religion into a social imagination. Charles Taylor sees in this kind of "disembedded religiosity" a necessary condition for the development of the modern social imagination by means of which people conceive themselves through horizontal connections.[3]

Simultaneity and extra-modernity

The narrative of modernity institutes a hierarchical relationship of distance in time and space between the center, that is, the European countries, and peripheral countries. The linear and evolutionary conception of time that underlies the theory of modernity establishes a mapping of the world that draws a binary opposition between modern and traditional peoples, between civilized peoples and barbarians, between developed and underdeveloped. The narrative of modernity not only describes the characteristics of countries that are developed but also establishes a hierarchical relationship based on a notion of progress that interprets change in terms of direction and considers it as a superior stage to which one must aspire. The ideal of progress feeds the universalist scope of modernity by encouraging other countries to follow it as a model of engagement and change.[4] The experience of modernity is not conceived of in a neutral or objective way: each country, each cultural area is evaluated in terms of its proximity or distance with respect to the modern notion of progress.

All studies on non-European countries are based on two theoretical presuppositions: a historical backwardness and a lack of modernity that obscure the configurations peculiar to modernity in these spaces.

The notion of time intrinsic to the theory of modernity is not independent of the identity-related constructs and hierarchical relations between the center and other countries. It amounts to an implicit denigration of the present time, of contemporaneity, of the simultaneity that non-Europeans experience. The use of time in constituting the relationship between self and Other is not neutral but on the contrary serves to interpret differences in terms of situation in time and of greater or lesser advancement in progress, what Johannes Fabian has called, the "denial of coevalness."[5]

But the problematic relation between modernity and time is also a characteristic trait of collective practices in non-European countries. The "progress" defended by Kemalist elites in order to "reach the level of contemporary civilization" clearly reflects this problematic relation to local and present time. The notion of "contemporaneization" (*çağdaşmak* in Turkish) designates a movement toward the future and expresses a desire to "become" contemporary, which is a synonym for "European," rather than a desire to be in the present time. Moreover, the argument that the state used in the 1990s to forbid wearing the Islamic headscarf in the universities—namely, that "the Islamic article of clothing is not in conformity with contemporary dress codes"—proceeds from this same identification of "contemporary" with the Western world.

Introducing the notion of present time, of simultaneity, allows us to more effectively decenter Western modernity and bring out the theoretical fecundity of extra-Western practices without reducing them to some kind of "historical lag," a phenomenon of "transition," or a lack of modernity. To constitute cultural areas as an object for the study of modernity, we have to put them into dialogue with the spirit of the time, instead of seeing in them a partial, incomplete version of modernity.

For all that, simultaneity does not in any way signify a similarity of experiences; on the contrary, it is a question of making intelligible the asymmetries of desires and trajectories between Europe and other parts of the world. A mirror effect of European modernity is an integral part of non-European histories. We have to see how it is reconstructed through time in different contexts, how some of these traits are privileged, accented, and others neglected. Rather than thinking in terms of a deficit of modernity, we have to talk about the configuration of extra-European modernity in terms of "extra," analyzed both as "external" to Europe and as a "plus," that is, as something that is added to modernity and not subtracted from it. I analyze this "extra" as both a reference to a trait of European modernity and as an over-investment of this trait, which becomes an invented, peculiar practice. In Europe, the advent of modernity means giving priority to the present time and breaking with the past.[6] The idea of a break with the past, a tabula rasa or "new life," is found in both Turkey and China. We can study it in asymmetrical terms but also as an "extra"; more than the valorization of the present, it is the radical devalorization of the past that seems to have structured the process of modernization in China and Turkey in accord with the European model elaborated at the beginnings of modernity.[7]

Let us take Turkish secularism as our example. Regarding a Muslim country, people tend to think in terms of a deficit of secularism; however, an analysis in terms of an excess of secularism is more capable of helping us understand the modern history of Turkey. Having emerged from a long positivist tradition, Turkish secularism is the main founder of Turkish nationalism; this authoritarian secularism, underwritten by the military, is also didactic (to adopt Ernest Gellner's formula[8]) insofar as it teaches and imposes a modern mode of life and modern behavioral patterns. Thanks to a secular education system, the Turkish republic was able to create its own elites. We can also analyze as a secular project the place given the question of women and their civil rights, with the abolition of Sharia and the adoption of the Swiss Civil Code. Women play a major role in the transmission of secularism as a way of life, women's public visibility being defined in opposition to the cultural codes of the Islamic religion, and especially to the veil and the segregation of the sexes.

Secularism concerns not only the institutional and juridical level but also shapes the "lower" level that Danièle Hervieu-Léger has called the level of the "civilizing base."[9] The role women have played cannot be understood without taking into account this cultural register that is part of the civilizational question. The notion of civilization leads us to Norbert Elias's definition of civilization as the West's sense of its own superiority as a superior model of life.[10] To put this in other words, although it is by reference to European civil society that secularism agitates the social and the social imagination in Turkey at the same time it takes singular, "extra" forms, this also means that it is outside the common, "extra-ordinary," capable of producing surprises, and thus we should attempt to understand it theoretically.

To come back to the debate about cultural areas, we can consider secularism as a question of the social imagination, which circulates, takes institutional forms, and gives rise to cultural practices that differ depending on the spaces and the historical context. From this point of view, it is not possible to make Europe a cultural area like others because it imposes itself as an unavoidable reference point for all other experiences. French secularism, seen as an exception, thus constitutes for Turkish modernization a model and an ideological reference point. An analysis in terms of social imagination whose objective is not to gauge Turkey's deviation from the ideal European "model" allows us to understand its own coherence in relation to secularism and its singularity with respect to the Muslim cultural area. Cultural areas help us understand the singularity of experience insofar as they bring out the historical and linguistic imprint that shapes the present.

Besides, secularism circulates in both directions: the project of organizing Muslim worship in France proposed by President Nicolas Sarkozy reminds us of the practices of Turkish secularism, which sought more to establish state control over religion than to promote its autonomy.

In summary, we have to reconsider the characteristics of modernity (mobility, the question of women, secularism, etc.) in their particular extra-European modalities, and this requires a bi-directional examination not only of the relations between European forms of modernism and extra-European spaces, but also and especially of the relations between non-European cultural areas—for example, by instituting a dialogue between Islamic studies and Subaltern studies.[11] It is not a matter of simply advocating an interpretation of modernity that seeks to decenter Europe in order to explode binary oppositions and open the field of reflection to "multiple modernities"[12] but also of bringing out what is peculiar to each cultural area and what passes in a horizontal way from one to the other. By shifting the center of gravity, by initiating an interpretation of modernity that is anchored in the multiplicity of cultural areas, we will at the same time breathe new life into the social sciences.

CHAPTER 8

Secularism, the Public Space, and Islamic Visibility

Turkey offers a choice terrain for the analysis of power relationships between secular and Islamist actors. Since the nineteenth century, by virtue of its past as a noncolonized nation, there has been in this country a strong and continuous tradition of leading elites that have sought to conduct a reformation of society, setting as their objectives its secularization and modernization on the Western model. We can say that today this project has succeeded in establishing itself in civil society as well as in the social imagination of many of Turkey's inhabitants, even if it has been repeatedly threatened by political Islam. As for Turkish Islam, it has enjoyed a certain power and even a political legitimacy, although intermittently and in a conflictual way, especially since the creation of the National Order Party (*Milli Nizam Partisi*) in 1970.[1]

Turkey is a terrain that is all the richer for the analysis of the meaning of this debate between secularism and Islam because the relation between them is established in a space that offers opportunities for public debate, for changes in leadership by means of elections, and a free market open to global commerce. Five major hypotheses run through the following developments:

1) Secularism, as the ideology at the foundation of the Turkish republican state, underlies the training and power of the Kemalist elites.

2) In Muslim contexts, secularism is equivalent to state control over the public space (whence the use of a loanword based on French *laïcité* rather than on English "secularization") and to the exclusion of Islam

from the public space. Secular principles are implemented by authoritarian prohibitions.

3) Secularism is not solely the official ideology and the work of the established political elites: it is also a value shared by a major part of civil society. To borrow the title of Cornelius Castoriadis's book,[2] it is part of the "social imagination." Thus the cleavage does not divide the state and the society vertically but traverses all social classes and concerns diverse institutions and milieus.

4) Public spaces become sites where this debate between standardizing secularism and the Islamism of difference can take place.

5) New Islamist actors, independently of their will and their declared intentions, do not themselves escape this process of secularization.

Secularism and the production of the republican elites

In Turkey, secularism and positivism have been the two pillars of the project of modernization that was begun in the nineteenth century and led to its being established institutionally and ideologically in 1923. Both secularism and positivism, which in the West are chiefly products of politics and science, acquired in Turkey a particular meaning and function in the adoption of the modernist project in a Muslim and non-Western country. Positivism underlies a conception of universal modernity insofar as it defines a rational and scientific mode of thought and a stage of progress at which every society must someday arrive. As a result, positivist ideology detaches Western modernity from its cultural and religious basis and thereby legitimates the modernization (and even Westernization) efforts made by the elites of non-Western countries. Since the "Young Turks," the secular vision of history forged by the positivism of Auguste Comte has provided a frame of reference for Turkey's progressive elites. Moreover, the Saint-Simonian view of society, the ideology of social engineering, a corollary of positivism, has defined the elites' mode of action in their effort to implement a rational society. The positivist theme of "progress and order" explains the priority given to the "national order," without which, according to modernist Turks, no secular reform can be carried out in a Muslim country.[3] Thus it is French Jacobinism, a centralist model of change, rather than Anglo-Saxon liberalism, that serves as a model for Turkish modernists.

And it is French republican "laicité," national secularism, rather than Anglo-Saxon liberalism that serves as a model for Turkish modernists—as the common use of *laiklik*, a Turkish version of the French word *laicité*, shows. Another way of distinguishing the two models is to say that one gives priority to "freedom from religion" whereas the other gives priority to "religious freedom." Consequently, secularization appears to be a political project rather the result of a social development—whence the common use of the Turkish version of the French word *laïcité: laiklik*.

Nonetheless, in Turkey secularism has followed a quite different path from that of its French model.[4] In France, it is characterized by the progressive separation of state and church, the neutrality of the state with regard to religions, and the secularization of the public sphere. In Turkey, on the other hand, religious matters are not autonomous but regulated by the state. Secondly, we cannot speak of state neutrality with regard to other religious and denominational groups because Sunni Islam represents, although only tacitly, the "official religion" (hence the criticisms of non-Muslim minorities as well as other Muslim denominational groups.

It is only regarding this secularization of the public sphere that a certain similarity appears. The controversy over the Islamic headscarf (*türban meselesi*) that has taken place in Turkey and in France testifies to this. It shows the parallel between the two conceptions and above all reveals the central place occupied by the questions of education and women in the debate over secularism. In France, the headscarf issue has been connected with questions of immigration and multiculturalism, and at first the problem concerned the secondary schools.[5] Female Muslim students' demand that they be allowed to wear the Islamic headscarf within universities and public high schools aroused strong reactions among *laïcs* in both countries, who see in this an assault on public education, women's rights, and republican principles.

The secularization of the public space and the suppression in it of religious practices and symbols (such as crosses in schools and courtrooms) are important aspects of French *laïcité* that were gradually established in the course of the democratization that took place during the Third Republic.[6] In Turkey (as in other Muslim countries) secularism is considered to be the *sine qua non* for modernity rather than for democracy.[7] In the public space as a site where modernity must be displayed, every religious practice and sign is eliminated, religious sects are outlawed, officials must conform to dress codes, and the music to be played on radio and television is prescribed. Secularism as a modernist ideology goes hand in hand with authoritarian state practices intended to control the public space. These practices, which were rigid in the early days of the Turkish republic, especially during the period of one-party rule from 1923 to 1946, and which became more flexible with the democratization begun in 1950, still find favorable terrain confronted by political Islamism. Turkish secularity is, as Ernest Gellner put it, a "didactic secularism."[8] It is moralizing and pedagogical, seeking to teach, and impose, a secular and thus modern way of life.

The model of Turkish secularism has led to radical institutional changes in matters relating to government and the legal system. We can mention in particular the abolition of the Caliphate in 1924; the suppression of the Ministry of Religious Foundations; the abolition of religious courts and titles; the adoption of the Swiss criminal code in 1926; the proclamation of the republic as a "secular state" in the 1937 constitution. But alongside these changes at the level of the state, the bureaucracy, and the law, secularism also played an important role in the training of the republican elites.

First of all, a system of education that was national and rational proved decisive in this training. The state's monopoly on teaching (all educational institutions having been put under the authority of the minister of education in 1926) did away with the official recognition of religious teaching and established the supremacy of secular, modern education on the national level. The advent of the nation-state was thus accompanied by the centralization of education and the training of new national elites. Furthermore, the replacement of the Arabic alphabet by the Latin alphabet (1928) and the attempts to expunge Persian and Arabic influences in the Turkish language in order to return to the origins of the "pure Turkish language" (*öztürkçe*), under the guarantee and supervision of an Institute of Turkish Language (*Türk Dil Kurumu*) created in 1932, established a radical break with the past and the old Ottoman elites. Linguistic and scriptural reforms initiated a symbolic and literal (*verbatim*) shift toward Western civilization. The adoption of the Latin alphabet helped consolidate the choice to secularize. Thus Turks were cut off from the language of the Qur'an, and their connection with the Arab and Muslim world in general was broken. In their efforts to "demythify" religion, the republican elites encouraged the translation of the Qur'an and public prayers in Turkish.[9] Today, prayer in Turkish has once again become a subject to be fought over in public debate.

The republican elites are thus pure products of a new way of writing, reading, and speaking. The use of the Latin alphabet, the practice of the original Turkish, without local accent, the mastery of foreign languages (English gradually winning out over French), reference to Western science and literature—all these traits distinguish the secular republican elites. They apparently feel no regret at being cut off from their Ottoman past, perhaps because they consider the cultural legacy too burdensome and see in it an obstacle to their desire to turn toward the future, that is, toward the West. And since their raison d'être is linked to the nation-state, these new elites are faithful agents of the reproduction and transmission of Kemalist values of progress.

The secularization of everyday practices and the public space is as important as education in the fabrication of the republican elites. The adoption of the metric system and the Gregorian calendar, the celebration of the new year, and especially the establishment of Sunday as a holiday, along with civil marriages, are among the striking examples of the secular modernism implemented in the everyday organization of time and social practices. Finally, for a Muslim society, the place of women in everyday life is the most significant result of secularization. Women appear as symbols and central agents in the transmission of the secular values embodied in ways of life.

Public space, women's space

The penetration of secularism in everyday practices is manifested in the visibility of women on the bodily and societal levels. That is why, in most Muslim countries, women's abandonment of the Islamic veil represents a great advance in the direction of progress and modernity. In other terms, in a Muslim context, secularism defines a modern way of life calling upon women to free themselves from religion, given concrete form in the veil and the segregation of the sexes. Women's participation in public life as citizens and government officials, their visibility in urban spaces, their socializing with men, all indicate a secular way of life and an important change in the way civic life is organized and in the behavior of the sexes with respect to the context of the Islamic religion.[10]

Perhaps the most tenacious difference between the Western world and the Muslim world lies in the definition of the private sphere and the identity of women. The private, which has no synonym in Muslim culture, refers to the closed sphere, the interior, intimacy, but also to a sphere that is sacred, gendered, and forbidden (for male outsiders) and best expressed by the term *mahram*. The Islamic veil recalls the prohibition on a woman being seen by any man external to her family, but it also marks the borderline between the inside and the outside and symbolizes the segregation of the sexes.

To put it metaphorically, Kemalist reformism sought to destroy precisely this *mahram* and provide women access to public life. We can even say that what was to define the democratic stake in the public space was the visibility of women. If in each revolution we find the "new man," for Kemalism it was more a question of the "modern woman." The touchstone of secularism is the status of women. Considering this interest in women's rights, we can more easily speak of the feminist nature of Kemalism than of its democratic nature. Kemalist modernization finds its meaning more in the construction of feminine citizenship than in the civil rights of citizens. It is to be noted that such a trajectory differs considerably from that of the West, where the emergence of the public space was realized with the exclusion of women from civil rights.[11]

In Turkey, a non-Western country that has deliberately engaged in modernity, the public space has become an extremely ambivalent place because it is loaded with the symbolic and political dimension of modernity. The political stake in the debate between Islamists and secularists is based, then, on the definition and habitations of the places of modernity. University campuses, seats in parliament, concert halls, beaches, television channels, all take on a dimension simultaneously symbolic and real, and the Islamists are challenging the secular occupation of these spaces. The definition and control of public space is becoming one of the main issues over which Islamist and secular actors are struggling. Political Islam is challenging the secular borderlines of the public space, breaking its homogeneity and aiming at an Islamization of ways of life and public behaviors. The recent appearance of the Islamic headscarf in the Turkish parliament is an illustration of this.

The debate on the Islamic headscarf, which in Turkey concerns chiefly higher education and thus university campuses, took a different direction after the general elections of 1999, when, for the first time in the history of Turkish democracy, Merve Kavakçi, a thirty-one-year-old woman elected as a representative of the pro-Islamic party, entered the National Assembly wearing an Islamic veil, even if for only a few hours on the legislature's opening day, May 2. Her career corresponds to the same social dynamics as that of the women I have studied who are Muslim and modern.[12] But at the same time, she is almost too representative of an American and global view of modernity. Having lived in the United States for a long time and holding a degree from the University of Texas in engineering and computer science, divorced from a Jordanian-American husband and the mother of two children, Merve Kavakçi had been, ever since returned home (about four years earlier), a member of the pro-Islamic party in Turkey. The fact that she had lived in the United States and her mastery of English and new technologies became symbols of modernity, a proof that "Muslims" were also taking advantage of modernity, when necessary and that they also had elites similar to the secular, Westernized elites. This fact burst upon, and caused a scandal in, the space carefully limited and regulated by the secular republican ideal. It was within this framework that the new representative's discourse and attitude broke. But if on the one hand the headscarf recalls premodern conceptions of women, of the individual, and of space, this polysemy of signs created confusion among Muslims as well as among secular people.

Merve Kavakçi broke the frame, challenged unwritten secular parliamentary rules, and destabilized the domination exercised by secular women. She seems no less modern than Turkish women whose attitude is modeled on the secular, national public sphere. In defending themselves, feminists, disconcerted by her attitude, choose to give priority to secularism over the identity of women. Her headscarf, a symbol of her difference inscribed on her body, is a problem. Secular feminists, among others, became "modern" women by taking off their headscarves. They see themselves as modern first of all in their bodies, the way they dress, their way of life, before they take into consideration the abstract category of citizenship. They are the product of a historical, emotional, and bodily break with Muslim identity that has led them to become modern. They can no longer turn back. They will defend the republic's secular achievements, their rights as modern women, if necessary physically.

It is certainly true that the headscarf is a political symbol, but the difficulty is precisely that it is no longer worn by older women but rather by active, competitive young women who insist on being included in the space of modernity. Merve Kavakçi, like the other women, disturbs people because she is Muslim and modern, refusing to choose between her two identities. We could just as well say that she is neither Muslim nor modern. Her way of reintroducing religiousness into the spaces of secular modernity expresses a resistance to assimilation, a criticism of modernity, whereas her personal career, despite her intentions, does not escape the process of secularization. By her profession as a computer engineer, her mastery of English, and her independence, she incarnates the rational, technical, individualist, and cosmopolitan values of modernity. To the extent that the rational and individual mode of thought emerges as an autonomous space through education and profession, and where there is a separation of the sacred and the profane, we can indeed say that a process of secularization has begun. Paradoxically, Islamist elites do not escape republican ideals; they are almost inverted doubles of them.

It remains to discover whether, once the homogeneity of the public space has been broken, democratic rules of consensus can be established. How secularism can free itself from republican ideology and cease to be the prerogative of a part of society to become a shared value of democracy, not only in practices but also in the collective consciousness. and how the question of multiculturalism and difference can be grasped in a context of Muslim modernity. If the public space is freed from state control, it can become a place for democratically recognizing cultural and religious differences just as much as a place of fragmentation and division. How can we avoid crumbling into pieces, on the one hand, and authoritarianism on the other? The power relationships between Islamists and secularists raise questions common to various modern societies.

CHAPTER 9

Questions of Women, Questions of Civilization?

In the late 1970s, as a young doctoral candidate in Alain Touraine's team, I was working on feminist movements in France. In the context of that research, I had to interview some members of these movements who, to my great surprise, suggested that I join them at the *hammam* (steam bath) of the Paris Mosque, in the fifth arrondissement. Somewhat embarrassed, I wondered whether it was my being an "oriental woman" that had led them to choose such an informal place. It was only later that I realized that the *hammam* had become one of the places that feminists of that generation had appropriated for themselves, and which their imagination prized as an exclusively feminine space. We must not forget that in women's construction of their identity, to be among other women, away from men's eyes, was at that time to develop a "sorority" that represented a crucial stage in the emancipation of women.

For my own part, my upbringing had not made me particularly familiar with the rites of the "Turkish bath," and that was an additional reason for feeling intimidated by the suggestion made by these French feminists. For the generation and the social milieu of a woman like my mother, the *hammam* already occupied a central place in socializing, but it was marginalized by the desire to adopt a modern way of life, which was then synonymous with the Western way of life. The way I was looked at made me uneasy: being a Turkish woman yet so little familiar with a place spontaneously associated with oriental women!

But life in the oriental fashion had lost much of its attraction for Turkish women since Western-style life had been seen as a superior model corresponding to modernity. Thus the private bathroom, a synonym of social prestige, had profoundly altered social habits, the notion of hygiene replacing collective care for the body: the morning shower, a symbol of efficient individualism, had gradually established a new temporality of cleanliness in everyday life.

Westernization had in fact penetrated everyday life, transforming habits, the relationship to the body and caring for oneself, shifting the borderlines between the individual and the collective, and rearranging the spaces of sociability and private life with new objects that had come from the context of European-style life. The appearance of the individual bathtub in apartments still remains the quintessential sign of the entry into modernity for all "oriental" cities, including both Teheran and Istanbul, even though this piece of equipment is often diverted from its initial use to serve as a reservoir in case of a water shortage. At the same time, the *hammam*, which has entered into Western customs, continues to spread in Western cities, and it is now found in the new form of "steam cabinets" in athletic clubs and beauty parlors.

Civilization and practices of civility

Why are the practices, ideas, ways of life, and clothing styles belonging to a given culture prized and even adopted by other cultures, or, on the contrary, disdained and rejected? Exchanges among cultures, the movement and circulation of objects, ideas, and men and women in different contexts require a comparative interpretation that can bring out the meanings, diversions, and misunderstandings that underlie these connected histories. Even if there is exchange, a movement in both directions and not in one alone, it is still the narrative of modernity that has authority and that hierarchizes practices and values.

It is not a "free" trade that governs the action of modernity but rather a universal aspiration to distinguish oneself as "civilized." The narrative of modernity is based on the postulation of a universal history, on the promise of a progress shared by the whole of humanity, and thus nourishes the ambition to interpret the whole of human experience.[1] We cannot understand the impact of modernity on other cultures without emphasizing its universal vocation. But this universalism is also borne by a characteristic of civilization, by a pretension to a superior way of life that makes Western men (and women) more "civilized" than others, that is, than the "barbarians."[2] This notion, which functions in dichotomies, hierarchizes differences between values and practices while at the same time binding them to one another. Every practice, no matter what its cultural and geographical origin, is henceforth caught in the interpretive nets of this dichotomy. Consequently, we cannot speak of distinct civilizations; all civilizations are concerned, transformed, and hierarchized by the horizon of modernity. In the past it was through the processes of colonization and Westernization, and now it is through the phenomena of immigration and globalization, that the codes of modernity have traversed and continue to traverse national, cultural, and geographical borderlines and participate in the subjective construction of social meaning.

The contrast between these necessarily interwoven notions of the civilized and the "barbarian" recapitulates, in a derived form, the opposition between the West and Islam (among other things), at the heart of which stands the question of women. The subjectivity that is the most significant, the most visible, but also the most revealing from the point of view of alterity, is the one that has to do with the domain of women. Modern societies are defined and transformed by the principle of equality, which does not fail to have repercussions on the uses of the body, the organization of internal and external spaces, and the arrangement of the spheres of the private and the public. For Muslim societies, the equality of men's and women's rights and the public visibility of women imply a process of secularization and an abandonment of religious law, but also a different way of using the body (for example, unveiling) and space (the end of gender segregation). Questions of identity are relayed by their transcription in laws but also by their translation in the uses of the body and of space. An essential part of the question of civilizational differences revolves around women, for they crystallize ethnic difference in the concrete forms constituted by uses of the body and spatial segmentations. Women are not only markers of intercultural difference but also the link connecting civilizational difference with its translation to the reduced scale of concrete forms of civility.[3]

Norbert Elias provides an analytical approach that allows us to connect the notion of civilization with the study of the practices of civility.[4] Elias studies the transformation of manners, the history of social norms (shame, embarrassment, modesty, etc.) and the constant interaction between social constraints and emotional structure, *sociogenesis* and *psychogenesis,* to use his terms. Thus we can consider the civilizing process as a system of social norms and a codification of behavior that are gradually "incorporated" by individuals and felt to be natural. The civilizing process participates in the production and training of the civilized person. The modern attitude is thus defined by a series of "good behaviors" that are the "expression of the Western consciousness" and of national pride.[5] However, as Elias points out, the notion of civilization does not acquire the same meaning for all Western countries. The German national elites gave priority to the notion of "culture," defended "authentic virtue" and German language and literature, and reproached the country's aristocracy for imitating the "deceptive courtesy" of the French. Unlike Germany, France and England share the same sense of the term *civilization,* which in their case concerns only modes of social behavior. When we say that a person is "civilized," we are evaluating his social quality, his urbanity, his way of living, his mastery of the language, the way he dresses, his way of conducting himself in society.[6]

Two aspects of Elias's approach seem to me important for our investigation here. First, as the comparison between France and Germany suggests, the idea of a tension between cultural identity and civilization. This tension is not specific to these two countries, but traverses the intellectual debate that accompanied the process of the Westernization of extra-European countries (such as Turkey or Japan), a debate that is now being revived in contemporary societies with the advent of movements connected with ethnic identity and religion. Second, the idea that civilization is a set of manners, a code of civility, that designates and qualifies ways of being and living in society. Such an approach to the notion of civilization helps us move from one level to another, to connect the macroscopic level of civilizational spaces with the microscopic level of individuals and their relationship to civility. In today's social sciences, the notion of civility is neglected, perhaps simply because it makes us think of good manners, politeness, and hence of the submission of the individual to etiquette and conventions, whereas the new stage of emancipatory modernity emphasizes the quest for authenticity and sincerity.[7] Social norms can evolve and change meaning: dissimulation ceases to belong to the register of politeness, modesty becomes an impediment to freedom. And there again, norms of freedom and emancipation continue to pass through the body, to be "incorporated," acquired through "technologies of the body."

Marcel Mauss draws attention to such "technologies" through which "men and women, society by society, in a traditional way, know how to make use of their bodies."[8] Thus he writes: "Habits vary not only with individuals and their imitations, but also especially with societies, upbringings, conventions, fashions, and kinds of prestige."[9] It is the "social notion of the *habitus*" that interests him, and it is through the observation of these technologies of the body among sexes, ages, and cultures that he begins his study of societies and their differences. Relating a personal anecdote, Mauss observes, regarding ways of walking, how fashion and prestige affect the uses of the body: "A kind of revelation came to me in the hospital. I was sick in New York. I wondered where I had seen girls walking the way my nurses did. I had time to think about it. I finally realized that it was in the movies. When I got back to France, I noticed, especially in Paris, the frequency of that way of walking; the girls were French, and they also walked in that way. In fact, thanks to the movies, American ways of walking were beginning to arrive in France."[10]

In this anecdote, which he does not develop further, Mauss, bringing an anthropologist's perspective to bear on the techniques of walking, notes how, through the mediation of the cinema, the bodies of young French women became the receptors of American styles. Thus we see the power of the cultural impact that works through fashion and prestige and that presides over new technologies of the body and over the learning of a new social *habitus*.

The quarrel between culture and civilization

This detour leads us back to our initial question regarding the central role played by women in the intercultural and intercivilizational. Both through the phenomena of fashion and through movements connected with ethnic identity, feminism, or religion, women's bodies are both actors and receivers. The Westernization movement of the 1920s and the Islamization movement of the 1980s both emphasize women as actors of identity and alterity. Paradoxically, it is by studying the experiences of modernity in Muslim or extra-European cultural areas that we can best account for the centrality of women as civilizational indicators.

In this regard, the history of Turkey is exemplary. We have seen earlier how as early as 1923 Kemalism sought to transform the Turkish political and legal system and also to establish itself as a civilizing project that could remodel customs, ways of life, and everyday behaviors and habits. Women were pioneers of this "new life." However, I do not want to linger here over this reforming period of secular modernization; instead, I want to examine the period that preceded it. All through the nineteenth century, before the advent of the republic, intellectual trends developed around the question as to what impact the Westernization of society might have on the manners and the status of women.[11] This debate is all the more instructive because it seems to echo contemporary problems raised by the Islamist movement, namely the modes of interaction and the conflicts of civilizations that crystallize around the question of women and the Islamic veil.

From the first attempts at modernization, which began in 1839 with the period of *Tanzimat* ("reforms"), down to the advent of the secular republic in 1923, the East-West dilemma has been reflected in the elaboration of two trends of thought concerning the impact of the West on the modernization of Ottoman society. The first trend includes those who maintained that it was necessary to preserve the cultural and moral heritage of the past, and thus to limit the influence of Western civilization to its material, technical, and administrative aspects. The second trend maintained that civilization forms a whole and that tradition had to be adapted to the modern world. Those who were convinced of the universality of Western civilization criticized arranged marriages and polygamy and argued for free love and for women's right to an education. For the traditionalists, on the other hand, relations between men and women had to remain in conformity with the rules of the religious law (Sharia) if one wanted to preserve spiritual values and morality. The differing interpretations of Islam regarding the status of women were the subject of a polemic between traditionalists and occidentalists that involved women as well—women such as Fatma Aliye, a writer of the period who interpreted Islam in her own way and attacked polygamy.

Thus it was in the course of the period that prepared the way for the advent of the secular republic that the critique of religious traditions developed, notably with respect to the legal status and the place in society of women, who thus found themselves at the heart of the quarrel between traditionalists and occidentalists. Some books testify to the importance given to the question of women. A work by Salahaddin Asim, *The Degeneration of the Turkish Woman or her Female-ization* 1950),[12] provides a radical critique of religious traditions, which, according to the author, places women not in the category of human beings but rather in that of "females" and thus keeps them subjugated and outside "civilization." By "female," he means woman considered solely as useful for pleasure and reproduction, a status he criticizes by defending the necessity of women achieving the rank of true "human beings." With unusual severity, he denounces the exaltation of the role of the wife and mother for the Turkish Muslim woman, emphasizing that she is both "entirely the slave, the sexual object of the man" and the caregiver for the children, or "the one who nurses like a cow, but is in no case a civilized human being, a social individual in her own right." He states that through the obligation to wear the veil, masculine domination "does not recognize the woman's personality," and expels her from society and civilization "in the name and to the advantage of the man." Salahaddin Asim is not the only one to have very clearly equated the abandonment of the veil with the emancipation of women from religious traditions and masculine domination. Cela Nuri Ileri, another reformist thinker, states in his book *Our Women* that, if we want to "have Turks progress, we have to begin with women's rights."[13] Or again Halil Hamit, for whom the accession of women to the ranks of humans goes along with that of society's rise to the level of civilization. In *Feminism in Islam, or Absolute Equality in the World of Women*, he wrote: "You must do everything to see to it that your children have a positive idea of women and you must bring them up with that idea. Your son must detest misogynists. Your daughter must know her rights and find the strength to defend herself."[14]

For advocates of the Westernizing trend, the notion of civilization has a universal, religious, and egalitarian meaning, values defined above all with regard to the status of women. For traditionalists, on the contrary, the possible link between civilization and the freedom of women can only be negative. The grand vizier Said Halim Pasha, worried about the disastrous influence that the revolution provoked by the 1908 Constitution had on women's behavior, opposed any liberalization with regard to women's rights. Thus he wrote in French: "No civilization has ever begun with freedom for women; on the contrary, it is proven incontestably that all civilizations have collapsed the moment that women have won total freedom."[15] In the eyes of the traditionalists, only Islamic morality is capable of effectively confining the dangerous wave represented by Western civilization, a "civilization of debauchery" and the bearer of permissiveness. For them, refusing to wear the veil constituted not only an outrage to religion but also a source of social unrest (*fitne*). Polygamy and the repudiation of wives were seen as practices in conformity with natural law and the interests of the family. For some writers, the education of girls is legitimate insofar as they are taught religion. In *The Ladies of the Constitution*, a work written by Mehmet Tahir, we read: "Instead of the great seriousness that used to characterize our women, today there is only a love of lace and ribbons, fashionable tight dresses."[16] Another writer, Derviş Vahdeti, accuses the "Young Turks" of not doing their duty as "guardians of Sharia" and women of abandoning the veil in the name of freedom: "Our women are gradually rejecting the veil; on the pretext that the Muslim is free, cabarets and bordellos are being opened."[17] Traditionalists were unanimous in thinking that society had to be protected from the moral crisis that the West was going through. According to them, imitating Western civilization meant change that was superfluous and, more seriously, might sap the foundations of society, which was based on religious traditions. Thus for Mehmet Akif, the imitation of the West upset even traditions, ways of living and being oneself: "Imitation of religion, imitation of customs, imitation of dress, imitation of salutations, imitation of language. In short, a total imitation: a nation constituted not of human beings but of apes, that is what is not possible, because they cannot form a genuine, durable social body."[18]

This quarrel between Occidentalists and traditionalists, reproduced here very succinctly, clearly illustrates the centrality of women in the establishment of social choices. The notion of civilization—that is, Western civilization—acquires for the reformers of the time the meaning of a "new life." According to Peyami Safa, a thinker well-informed about the transition to modernity, Occidentalism is, "confronted by religious intolerance, the longing for progress that arises from the intuition of civilized needs." In a work entitled *An Occidentalist's Dream*,[19] the civilized world is described as one relieved of religious conservatism, "where women can dress as they like, where the police, religious fanatics and coachmen can no longer have any say about what women wear." The secular, modern "new life" is defined here at the level of "micro-practices," of an everyday life where people are free to choose their clothes and how to use their bodies. Women represent pioneers of this new life. Through the choice of their clothes, but also by their visibility in new spaces, they incarnate Western-style life. The traditionalists, on the other hand, are worried about the "suppression of the harem" as the end of the segregation of the sexes that can only lead to free contact between men and women, on the Western model. Thus they denounce "dancing, taverns, houses of prostitution, bars, theaters, and other such establishments" that pave the way for illicit relations between the sexes.

Atatürk's Republic, which this intellectual debate in a way prepared, gave this "new life" priority over any other model, thus putting an end to the conflict, which went back to the end of the eighteenth century, between culture and civilization. The republican "new life" signified the modernization of the social fabric, a change in customs, the investment of new places, the acquisition of new cultural habits, and the learning of new aesthetics and technologies of the body.

But it was mainly in the relations between the sexes that this change in mentalities and everyday practices made itself felt. The conception of the couple was idealized, as opposed to the model of the extended family and still more to the social segregation of the sexes: going for a walk, couples getting together, *en famille*, to use the expression fashionable at the time, dancing in couples (especially the waltz, at balls organized to celebrate the anniversary of the foundation of the republic), became the "exemplary" practices of a "civilized" way of life. What appears to us natural or obvious in a given culture takes on a very different meaning when it is transposed into other contexts. Marcel

Mauss pointed out, for instance, that "dancing cheek to cheek is a product of modern European civilization."[20] In a Muslim context, Western dancing acquires an additional meaning insofar as it marks a break with traditional modesty, introduces physical contact between men and women, and presupposes women's emancipation—all changes that mark the adoption of the modernist doctrine in order to count among the "civilized nations." This evolution in customs is part of a process of secularization and even signifies an "exit from religion," as Marcel Gauchet has described it.[21]

On the other hand, the liberation of the individual and the emancipation of the sexes are defined by reference to the cultural model of the West, which amounts to saying that the "civilized person" is the Westerner. But even today, although *individuals'* ways of life and modes of behavior are meticulously classified and hierarchized in accord with binary oppositions such as "civilized/archaic," "progressive/obscurantist," etc., it is incontestably regarding relations between men and women that these distinctions are the most striking. If at first only the elites adopted Western social norms, the middle classes later appropriated them during the whole history of the Turkish Republic, not only through education and urbanization but also through literature, film, and the media. Separated from their Western origins, these norms soon came to appear "natural."

The Islamization of customs, of bodies, and of space

It might be suggested that in an extra-European context, and especially a Muslim one, modernization follows a singular itinerary in which the process of secularization is closely linked, at least initially, with the Westernization of customs. It is difficult to grasp this historical singularity in the eminently cultural, indeed civilizational, sense of contemporary Islamic protest. The appearance of the Islamic movement forces us, in fact, to revise our interpretation of the history of modernization. The Islamic movement seeks nothing less than to reintroduce religion into the public space and to challenge Western customs. The debate about the opposition between culture and civilization gains new energy in the form of the tensions between identity and modernity, the question of women being once again at the heart of this societal debate. In this context, the issue of the veil always has to be discussed. The veil is the icon through which the Islamization of customs becomes public. It points to the new prohibitions (and the technologies) of the woman's body and highlights the difference of the sexes as the difference of civilizations. It is concerning the veil that the alterity between the Western world and the Muslim world becomes once again a subject of debate in terms of differences in civilization that echoes the intellectual debate that took place at the end of the nineteenth century. This debate is not limited to Muslim countries insofar as the resumption of the veil has crossed boundaries to become, as the controversy in France has shown, a European matter.

The politicization of Islam expresses the quest for identity among Muslims who are making their way through what modernity offers them. These Muslims have left the cities where they were born, they have been educated in republican schools, and they find themselves confronted by the demands of liberal modernity, both in large cities such as Istanbul and in the French suburban ghettos (*les banlieues*). If they clutch at the new values of Islam to define themselves, that is because they are involved in an ethnic identity-related process that—contrary to the first generation of Islamists—is infiltrating itself into the definition of customs, manifests itself in personal practices, is part of a performative activity, invests the public space, and thus acquires visibility and reflectiveness. Today, Islamic identity is defined less by a collective and discursive process than by a performative and personal one that seeks to inscribe it on the public space. The Islamization of customs pushes the *habitus* toward change and protest. In this sense, contemporary Islam proceeds in a way identical to that of modernism, because each of the two trends seeks to reach the micro-level of the construction of the subject and its social *habitus*. Thus the latter takes priority over the former and not the other way around, as many political scientists think. And it is by putting the question of woman at the heart of our investigation that we can "think differently, instead of thinking less," to adopt Irène Théry's remark,[22] and bring out the social domain of the *habitus* and the relationships between the sexes in the fabrication of the subject and of history.

To distance ourselves from European modernity is also to seek to show how this domain is regulated by a difference between the sexes and also by a political difference. Western thinkers who have dealt with the social *habitus*, customs, or the body pay hardly any attention to the sexual or the protest aspect, which become, however, prominent traits in intercultural approach. Only in extra-European contexts can we observe the impact of modernity in its "civilizational" aspect, that is, in the fabrication of the civilized subject, a fabrication that is both political (and even colonizing, in certain contexts) and sexual. In the same way, contemporary Islam proceeds in accord with an approach that is both sexual and political. While on the one hand it engages in an Islamization of the social *habitus*, of customs, and of the definition of the subject that crystallizes around the woman question, on the political level it establishes a new hierarchization of the values of modernity. The Islamization of customs reflects a will to separate oneself from the experience of modernity and Western values. But it is just this demand that raises the most problems and elicits a civilizational clash for everything that has to do with women. It is through the question of women that the orientation of the values of modernity becomes a civilizational stake. Not only the veil but also religious marriages, polygamy, the punishment of adultery, and lapidation become subjects of public debate even in Europe.

In other words, for contemporary Islam, it is not so much the entry into modernization that is at stake but rather the religious orientation of the ethical and aesthetic values of modernity. It is not a matter of a slow transformation of customs that takes place over the long term but on the contrary of an action on the part of Islamic actors that is performative, resolute, and reflective. The Islamic collective imagination acts on the scale of micro-practices, radicalizes the values of Islamic modesty, and improvises a new religiousness and personal discipline. In the context of pluralism, but also when faced with prohibitions, it is indeed a matter of improvisation. In Iran, women resist the obligation to wear the veil by finding ways to be "incompletely veiled," to reveal a little lock of hair, to shorten the length of the overcoat, to uncover themselves in "homeopathic" doses, as one of them put it.[23] Confronted by the Revolutionary Guards' supervision of morals, the woman's body is the stake in an everyday battle. In Turkey, where public space is, on the contrary, governed by the principle of secularism and where wearing the veil is prohibited in the universities, students get around this prohibition by wearing hats or wigs. These subversive practices have also been improvised in France since the National Assembly passed a law banning "ostentatious" religious insignia in the schools. Since the autumn of 2004, some girls have worn a "bandanna" that substitutes for the headscarf. The visibility of religious signs is becoming a major issue in the definition of the public space. The goal of these performative practices is to introduce religious difference into various public spaces such as schools, universities, streets, and public parks, along with swimming pools, hospitals, and the national legislature.

The public sphere and the private sphere

Although the public sphere is an abstract notion that refers to the rights of citizens and a common space, it is also a concrete, plural notion that covers the diversity of institutional and social spaces. The process of secularization, like that of Islamization, seeks to define the foundations of a common life, the public sphere, through secular jurisprudence in the former case, and through religious law (Sharia) in the latter case. But this public sphere is also defined by its relationship to the private sphere. Thus it is the boundaries between the two spheres that become a social issue. The feminist movement of the 1970s in Europe also challenged the boundaries between private and public spaces: the feminist leitmotif of "the personal is the political" expresses well the feminists' claim to reveal the forms of oppression that are hidden in the private sphere, to transpose them into the public sphere, and thus make them a political object of women's liberation. The Islamist and the feminist movements seek to redefine, in very different and even opposite ways, the values and the boundaries of the private and the public spheres. In both cases, the question of gender is central insofar as it is the point of contact between the private and the public. Secularization and equality of the sexes have become an inseparable pair in the definition of the Western feminist subject. That is precisely the central issue for the Islamic subject. It is crucial for the direction to be taken by the Islamic movement, because only the recognition of the equality of the sexes can transform Islamic radicalism, and it is equally crucial in the encounter between the West and Islam, between Europe and the Muslims.

To conclude, I would like to come back to the example of the Turkish bath. The Islamization of customs introduces new norms of conduct, new definitions of civility, such as prohibitions on contact between men and women, and between women themselves. Muslims who are looking for a purer, more fundamentalist form of Islam condemn nudity among women, appealing to the Islamic principle according to which women must expose their bodies before no one other than their husbands, and thus, attentive to their chastity, they prefer the private showers recently installed in some *hammams*.[24] The quest for a new Islamic modesty is also very attractive for young Muslim women in France and Germany. Those who are very devout try to respect and introduce the rules of modesty in swimming pools and also in traditional *hammams*. This involves not only the separation of the sexes but also the mode of covering (a "burkini" has been inventeda hooded swimsuit that covers the legs as far as the knees in order to hide the areas called *awra*, which must be hidden not only from men but also from other women).[25]

These examples show how contemporary Islam creates a new tension between popular traditions and more conscious and political interpretations of religious principles. Naturally, throughout the history of Islam, these popular traditions have been a subject of discord among theologians. Visiting public baths has thus been considered "non-Islamic," as has sometimes been harshly condemned by Islamic jurists. Although the baths have never been prohibited, some theologians have nonetheless advised men to forbid their women to go there. Thus in the Middle Ages, the great jurist Ibn al-Hajjaj condemned the *hammam* as a place that corrupted the principle of modesty: Muslim women did not respect the Islamic rule that the body should be covered from the navel to the knees, and, indecently, did not conceal themselves from the eyes of non-Muslim Christian or Jewish women who also visited these baths.[26]

Contemporary Islam certainly echoes the remarks of these traditionalist thinkers. But what makes it different is that the contexts in which Islam is not the hegemonic power but a minority religion in a secular and pluralistic setting allow and facilitate the reinvention or reinterpretation of these traditions by the actors themselves. Thus we can speak of an Islamization of customs, for here it is in fact a question of interpreting and incorporating and also of improvising rules of conduct between sexual individuals, of arranging space and training the body. It is no longer the institutions of Islam that govern religious practices but rather Muslims' search for a religious meaning in their personal and collective construction of the subject. Through these embodied, sexual practices inscribed on the training of the body and the arrangement of space, a certain way of living together takes form. It is only through an interpretation that puts woman at the center of the analysis and adopts a two-way perspective between Islam and the West, an intercultural perspective, that we can avoid the disembodied abstraction of the notion of civilization, which always masks and naturalizes power relationships in the domain of the social *habitus* and the definition of the values of civility.

CHAPTER 10

Publics, Republic, and Denied Citizenship

While keeping this symbol in the background, especially to refer to the "Islamization" of society and the "instrumentalization" of women, most political scientists who have worked on Islam have treated the question of the Islamic headscarf as an epiphenomenon. However, in my view, this question, far from being secondary, is central for understanding contemporary Islamism, and that is why it is so disturbing for the modern collective imagination. This collective imagination has to be deconstructed: in fact, relationships of subordination and domination have been established around the headscarf.

Islam and the public space: the question of women

During the first decade of Islamist movements, research regarding state control in the Muslim world was conducted with the goal of explaining the rise of political Islam by the failure of the elites' project of modernization on the political, economic, and ideological levels. Political scientists initially focused on authoritarian regimes in Arab countries and on the popular masses throughout the Muslim world who did not identify with the elites' project of modernization and who, in order to revolt against it, were supposed to be falling back on what they knew best, Islam. The vertical idea was that of a confrontation between the state, the established regime, and a fanatical and fundamentalist popular mass in revolt. In this framework, the question of the headscarf could only be an epiphenomenon insofar as the only serious question was the political and institutional logic, as in the case of the Iranian revolution.

Later on, political scientists finally realized that the question was not purely political and economic in nature, limited to a nation-state, a region (the Middle East), the Muslim world, or Muslim civilization, because it also emerged in the European public space, particularly in France. This emergence took place because it was concerning the headscarf—that is, women—that the debate crystallized and was radicalized. In public debate about Islam, women, as actors or non-actors, appear as the blind spot that causes a problem and all the more because the question of Islam no longer seem reducible to economic and political causes but instead manifests itself in its full cultural dimension. Thus we can ask whether it is not through this blind spot represented by women that the question of the headscarf can be analyzed in terms of social relationships of domination, hierarchy, etc., on the condition that we adopt a theoretical approach that takes into account the configuration of the public space and not solely the nation, the state, the political system, and the prefiguration of the "best regime."

Let us take a few empirical examples in order to adopt a two-way perspective and shift the debate by broadening it to cases that are not limited to France, in order to distance ourselves somewhat from the very French problematics of colonization and immigration. Approaching the problem in a transversal way, bringing in different contexts, can in fact provide us with new elements for analysis.

The first observation to make is that the emergence of Islam in the public space crystallizes around the question of women. In Morocco, for example, the monarchy's proposed bill establishing a new family law put in question polygamy, the repudiation of wives, the control over the choice of a woman's husband exercised by her father and brothers, and the setting of the legal age for marriage at fifteen for girls and eighteen for boys—all of which are rules inspired by religion. This is clearly an attempt to detach law concerning women from the strictly religious area and to define it by the political domain, even though the reform is explicitly based on Islamic sources. We see here that equality of the sexes involves a secularization of the law, and we find again a correspondence between the question of secularism and that of the equality of the sexes as it is posited in other contexts such as France and Turkey.

Another example: in 2003, the Nobel Peace Prize was awarded to Shirine Ebadi, who as an attorney had worked for the reform of family law in Iran, particularly as regards divorce and inheritance rights for women. Trained as a judge, she was no longer able to practice her profession after the 1979 revolution and began to be politically active as a lawyer. We see here again the connection between women's rights and democratization, a connection that the reformers also made. This example also shows that the social imagination of modernity, which now involves the equality of the sexes, is not limited to the European space: Shirine Ebadi is only and simply Iranian; she has hardly any acquaintance with foreign languages and has not attended any Western school—in short, she is a pure product of Iranian history and society and yet she is fighting for the equality of the sexes. Moreover, she is not alone: Islamic periodicals, edited by Muslim women who are more veiled than she is, are also fighting for women's rights.

A second observation: we must not think that these values do not circulate—what was true for nationalism at the beginning of the twentieth century is true today for the equality of the sexes and human rights. But in this case we can even summarize the situation, somewhat provocatively, by saying that "women's rights in the Muslim world are more important than human rights," as I tried to show for Turkey in my book *Musulmanes et modernes*.[1] All over the Muslim world we see that women's rights are central in secularizing reforms when it is a matter of defining the cultural orientation of a society. That is what we see in Morocco, where the monarchy, which remains politically intelligent even while negotiating with civil society, may be granting rights to women only to better repress the Islamist movement. All Muslim countries have experienced this kind of power relationships that are articulated around the question of women.

Secularism, from Turkey to France

In Turkey, public debate has recently centered on the October 29 celebration of the secular republic: the president of Turkey did not invite to the official ceremony the wives of representatives of the Islamist party who wore the headscarf. This is paradoxical and astonishing: in a Muslim country with a government that comes from the ex-Islamist party and considers itself democratic-conservative, completely pro-European and liberal, wives wearing a little shawl over their heads are not invited to an official ceremony! Two years earlier, the question as to whether a representative wearing the headscarf could be allowed to enter the parliament had come up: an adult woman, democratically elected, was thrown out because at the end of a complex and interesting career, she was wearing the headscarf.[2] Today, the question has shifted to representatives' wives, and we may wonder, from a feminist point of view and with a certain irony, whether Turkish secularists would not prefer the wives to women representatives themselves. Islamist representatives may have seats in parliament, but it is the headscarf that has triggered a public debate.

This crystallization around the headscarf and its prohibition in parliament, in republican ceremonies, and in Turkish schools and universities, reminds us of the debate over the headscarf and republican principles in France. The terms of the debate in the two countries are very similar. Comparison and broadening the perspective helps us understand that what is at stake is not limited to secular education but concerns the very definition of the public space. We see how various places—schools, universities, parliament, hospitals, prisons, and workplaces—are becoming sites for the public involvement of Islam and consequently areas of conflict. What is defined as public space seems to be the heart of the question.

But let us return to France, where it was also the headscarf that launched the debate about secular education and secularism and questioned the definition of the public space. The institutional representation of the Muslim religion through the establishment of the Conseil français du culte musulman did not cause as many problems. However, from the point of view of the history of secularism in France, it was a genuine turning point so far as the relations between the state and a particular religion are concerned. It is the definition itself of secularism that has been changed, to the extent that this measure establishes public recognition and supervision of Islam. However, there was no passionate debate about this. Why did the institutionalization of the representatives of the mosques, because that was what was involved, not seem to arouse as much anxiety, as much turmoil, as the public visibility of the headscarf?

The debate in France is focused on the question of the headscarf, exactly as it is in Turkey, where Islamist members of parliament pose many fewer political problems than the headscarf itself. This forces us, on the theoretical level, to look into the relationships between space and body. The question of Islam reveals that our common world is not as discursive as Jürgen Habermas claims by always presenting the public sphere as the space where rational debate takes place. Here, it is the visual that is involved. The question of Islam in the public space is first of all the question of its visibility. It is the identifying inscription on the body and in space, the confrontation between this space defined as public space and thus as a place of gathering and regulation at the same time, and the inscription within it of a difference and a non-conformity, that raise a problem. Thus people do not hear the discourse of the veiled schoolgirls, not only because they don't want to hear it, but also because it is unnecessary to do so: these schoolgirls communicate non-verbally, through the symbol of the headscarf. Here we can adopt Erving Goffman's term *stigmata*:[3] what causes a problem is not so much the attribute in itself as the relationship of communication in which it comes into play. How is the veil perceived and what meaning should be given to it? Of course, it is possible that it will eventually become a fashion statement, but today we are still far from that.

Woman as the key to modernity

Muslim countries entertain much more varied relations to Islam than is usually said: Morocco offers a model of conservative monarchy; the Iranian Islamic Republic advocates an Islam that is far from conservative, having nothing to do with the official Islam of Saudi Arabia; Turkey offers an example of a secular republic that is far more authoritarian than France, and whose way of dealing with Islam France is now adopting.[4] But what has provoked so much passion among secularists? In these four very different configurations of the relationship between Islam and the public space (including France), the central stake is the appearance of women in public: that is clearly what poses a social problem.

Thus we see that in Muslim countries the question of women is far from secondary. In European countries, according to Habermas and all feminist theories, the question of women is secondary to the extent that it appears at the end of a process of emancipation.[5] On the contrary, if in Turkey women's political eligibility and right to vote was granted in 1930, almost at the same time with the United Kingdom and fourteen years earlier than France, that is because women's participation in the public life signified a secular and modern move in the eyes of the reformists. In Turkey's case, this strong political will to carry out change, a conversion in civilization, was not an outcome of Western colonialization.

In all these examples, the question of women crystallizes that of the relations between Islam and the West. Through this question, we enter into a relational logic that is both external (between Islam and the West) and internal (between Muslim societies), because the question of women is seen as a marker for an issue that involves civilization as much as society: the question of the veil is not new; all the movements of modernization, Westernization, or colonization took up the question of women as a nodal point. We can thus define the formula of modernization in the 1920s as an equation: the emancipation of women from religion equals the country's development. If emancipation involves an emancipation from religion, national progress is related to the equality of the sexes, to women's public visibility: that is the endogenous formula of modernity in Muslim societies.

We can say in another way that women are central to the definition of the nature of the relation between Islam and modernity, both during the period of modernization and during that of Islamization. During the 1920s, the period of modernization, which was synonymous with Westernization for the majority of Muslim countries, the "unveiling" of women represented a symbol of emancipation and modernity, but for anti-colonial movements such as that in Algeria, veiling represented a way of resisting the power of the colonizer. The re-adoption of the veil by young urban women took place in the post-1980 period, following the Iranian Islamic revolution. But here again the context differs. It can be imposed by the state and made compulsory in public. There are also contexts in which Muslim women themselves choose to adopt Islamic dress codes while affirming their participation in public life.

If women are the key, the question is who will take control of this key. The political power, the conservatives in Iran, or the reformers? The monarchy in Morocco? Or the missionaries of civilization, such as the current secular feminists in France? Or Muslim women themselves? Or everyone at once, entering into interaction to open or close the door between Islam and modernity? Even if we do not yet know the answer, we see emerging a public staging in which actors meet and interact in diversified public and cultural spaces.

If we now consider the question from the point of view of citizenship, it could be formulated as follows: who has a right to enter and act in the public space, and to constitute himself or herself as a social actor? This presupposes a critical examination of the modern definition of citizenship. The narrative of modernity (the notion of ideology is too rigid and too limited to comprehend this phenomenon) is based on the presupposition of a secular citizen who has relegated religion to the private sphere in order to become a "full-fledged" citizen. The quality of a social actor, the capacity for public agency, is accorded only to adults: first in connection with age, initially to men but not women, then in connection with a secularization of the individual, understood as both implied by secularism and implying it. A religious actor, and still less an Islamic actor, is not recognized. But here there is a problem. I am not referring to the closure of the political system and the problems of the recognition of difference, etc., that it implies. I refer to cognitive structures, our way of constructing the modern political subject.

As Habermas has clearly emphasized, two indispensable conditions have to be fulfilled in order to constitute the public space as a space of public debate: age and rationality. Islamism, by way of the veil, is addressing a very deep, perhaps even unconscious, criticism to this construction of the modern political subject that involves rationality and which today is crystallized in the figure of the emancipation of women. From this point of view, religion is seen as a phenomenon that runs counter to rationality, and the headscarf is seen as a humiliation. The Islamic headscarf is perceived as a symbol that signifies the denigration of the modern subject, because the latter is defined by individual freedom of choice, the rational capacity for action, and the emancipation of women.

Concerning women more specifically, we find ourselves facing a twofold negation: in the eyes of the public, Muslim women who wear the headscarf are situating themselves doubly in this noncitizenship. In France, the headscarf phenomenon is situated in this noncitizenship because it does not refer to women's freedom of choice, given the age of the girls wearing it, but rather to the idea of religious submission that underlies the veil. However, the contemporary veil is also a personal way of reappropriating the religious, which is not necessarily situated in the logic of the family's wishes or community pressures. From this point of view, the case of the Lévy sisters (who were expelled from school for wearing headscarves) seriously damaged a very widespread stereotype. I myself have written on several occasions that the new veils, the headscarves, create a certain discontinuity with the family and the traditional world of religion: these new veils correspond to a personal relation to religion that is not the product of families, or men, or fundamentalists, or *communautarisme*, to use a term in vogue in France.

Now that the theme of masculine oppression has been exhausted, a supposed community pressure on girls is invoked to account for their adoption of the headscarf without ever acknowledging that their relation to Islam is personal and that they can act on their own. A personal relationship does not mean that there is no inscription in a collective sphere of influence: one can be part of a movement by maintaining a personal relation with it, like Western feminists who do not belong to a political organization but who have a very personal relation to the feminist consciousness and to the discourse of emancipation, which has changed their relation to the private, to the body, and to men.

To explain this denigration, this nonrecognition of women's capacity for action, of the public act, of personal affirmation, of the existence of the Muslim subject, is already to be engaged in the criticism and reconstruction of the discourse of modernity, of the modern social imagination. If the headscarf question is so central, that is because with the intrusion of religiousness, it is in contact with the pillar of the cognitive structure of the public space constructed by the modern imagination, with rationality, and because it reveals its limits in terms of citizenship. If today it is the figure of women's liberation in the name of the equality of the sexes that the West considers most important, that may be because it is the most recent accomplishment in the process of deploying the principle of equality in the dynamics of Western societies. As François Furet has shown,[6] the passion for equality that has agitated the social imaginations of Western countries implies a principle of social transformation by instituting equality among races, citizens, nations, countries, and finally the sexes. The Islamic veil suddenly reappears at a stage of modernity in which the equality of the sexes, men and women but also heterosexuals and homosexuals, is deeply agitating Western societies. The principle of the equality of the sexes implies a construction of the relationship to oneself, of the relation to the body, and it is around this construction that the conflict revolves. The liberation of women is situated first of all in the body, and that is why it is concerning the body and its public presentation that the debate is so heated. The veil, contrary to the slogan "our bodies belong to us," recalls another use of the body, a use that limits the demand for autonomy. One of the blind spots in the debate and the conflict proceeds from the different uses that we make of the body, and the cultural orientations they convey.

Proximity and face-to-face confrontation: the public space

It is with regard to space that the question takes on all its meaning. We can say that the conflict grows more serious when it is a matter of sharing the same place: so long as the distance between Islamists and secularists was maintained in a clear way in all the contexts we have mentioned, there was no problem. The headscarf worn by the first generation of women immigrants, like that of their grandmothers, created no difficulties. When secular Turks say "we love our grandmothers' headscarf," that is because the latter did not go out of their houses, never left their grandmother's easy chair, never claimed access to spaces other than the family, communal space. The case is similar to that of women of the first generation of immigrants, who remained closed up in their houses and were much more traditional, much less emancipated, from the feminist point of view, and less integrated, living in the enclave of the community. This headscarf did not disturb anyone. But today, when veiled girls cross the borderlines of the private space without assimilating the implicit conventions of the secular public space, being guided by a different bodily discipline and a different personal discipline, this attitude arouses anxiety. Proximity in space, schools, workplaces, and also in parliament or official ceremonies, turns into a face-to-face confrontation.

But this proximity also reflects, on the part of Muslim actors, an ambivalence that is all the more profound because the veiled girls do not resemble the women of the first generation of immigrants. Contrary to the latter, as feminine actors and Islamists, they situate themselves in a double logic, enjoy a double cultural capital, to paraphrase Bourdieu, at once religious and also secular and scientific. They can circulate in several spaces and present themselves in public. They have assimilated the disciplines and know how to navigate the schools, and even the political system, which gives them a double legitimacy, or a double illegitimacy, because in a certain way they leave the community and distance themselves from the traditional world of Islam while at the same time manifesting their disagreement, without going so far as to assimilate all the implicit conventions of modernity. Unlike their parents, they have cut their ties with their country of origin and with its traditions so that in them we see a de-ethnicization of religion. Contrary to what is generally thought and said, Algerians in France or Turks in Germany have a means, by becoming Muslims, of escaping the determinism of the colonial past or being classified as an illiterate immigrant who has no access to education in his new country. Already being situated in a logic of distantiation with respect to their country of origin and to their family, they are nonetheless not involved in a process of assimilating the cognitive structures of Western modernity.

That is what we see in particular with women, according to a process I have tried to account for with regard to Turkey in my book *Musulmanes et Modernes*. This double affirmation is at the same time a double negation, because saying that one is "neither entirely a traditional Muslim woman nor entirely a French European or modern person" is profoundly ambivalent, and it is this ambivalence that leads to anxiety because we cannot grasp it in black and white terms, in terms of "we versus they." This situation, which nevertheless involves a certain kind of hybridization, provokes defensive reactions that show the need to maintain borderlines. But the boundaries that are really involved here are those of the public space, within which the main issue is the degree to which otherness is accepted.

Related to the public space, the question cannot be reduced to the recognition of alterity alone, insofar as the latter can be maintained in a state of exteriority. It obliges us to include alterity and makes problematic the identity and definition of the public space, in this case that of France and of Europe. Turkey's candidacy for admission to the European Union has thus played a role identical to that of the veil and has led to a societal debate on European identity, as if, once the Turks had been taught a lesson, defenses against Muslims were erected, with this need to remind people of their common secularism when faced with the headscarf, to the point of conflating secularism and integration, and especially the necessity of setting limits to cope with an intrusion or even an invasion.

A final point that is a little more political and theoretical: are the republic and the public space one and the same thing? Making the public space autonomous with respect to the state is considered a condition for moving beyond state authoritarianism. In Iran, where the public space is placed under the supervision of the state and the hegemony of Islam, the battle for the autonomy of the public space is fought every day, waged in the streets by "incompletely veiled" women and young people who do not respect religious rules of behavior. Where does the borderline between the public space and the space of the state lie? In Turkey, the overlapping of these two spaces is much more limited, and we consequently note an autonomy of the public space that can be observed in the diversity of ways of life and the pluralism of politics and the media. However, the debate over the Islamic veil shows that state control and the stamp put by the Republic on the public space are still present.

There is a relationship between the notion of public space and the democratic ideal insofar as the latter allows a common space for gathering and opening up to which every citizen ideally has access. But through the study of Islam, this space encounters prescriptive limits that are also synonymous with closure and exclusion. Today, the emergence of the Islamic subject in the contemporary world reveals the limits of this public space and its interconnection with the republic. In France, the debate over the veil has increased the convergence of the public and the republic, it being taken for granted that they are virtually synonymous. Bruno Latour, in an article that is in tune with what I am trying to show, states that "public" signifies almost the contrary of "republic."[7] According to him, the "republic" is already constituted, as is "secularism," and today, the "equality of the sexes," thanks to feminist discourse. All these notions are incarnated by the state, the government, but they also have a consensual base among intellectuals, feminists, the bureaucracy, the schools, and teachers. The "public" is the whole created by our actions, sometimes actions that are partly conscious, but which nonetheless belong to the sociological subject, that is, to a subject whose actions have unexpected, unprecedented, paradoxical, or ambivalent consequences. How to take these into account? I think that reflecting on the basis of the "public" and not the "republic" opens up a space for reflection. To pay attention to the "public" is to explore, as Bruno Latour says, certain paradoxical or ambivalent aspects. It is researchers' task to inaugurate the debate in order to understand the meaning of these ambivalences, of these paradoxical practices, and thus to bring out the "public" in the "republic."

CHAPTER 11

The Veil, the Reversal of the Stigma, and the Quarrel over Women

The Islamic veil, which has been the contemporary symbol of Islamic piety and religious revivalism in Muslim societies since the end of the 1970s, appeared in other contexts in the 1980s, notably among the daughters of Muslim immigrants to Europe, and it launched the debate on the limits of multiculturalism and the recognition of the fact of religion.[1]

It was in France, starting in 2002, that this debate was expanded to the national level, leading all the intellectuals representing the political class and various associations, as well as the spokespersons for feminism, to express their opinions on the topic. The sudden appearance of the veil in schools, and within a society in which the values of secularism (proudly defended as a French exception) and equality of the sexes prevailed, provoked a trend in public opinion in favor of its interdiction. People who had previously had nothing to do with each other joined together to defend simultaneously two principles that had up to that point been separate, secularism and the equality of the sexes, principles that came to be interwoven and erected as ramparts against religious fundamentalism. In the course of this same debate, the term *headscarf* (*foulard*) was gradually replaced by that of *veil* (*voile*), a term that refers more explicitly to Islam. Despite a certain reluctance to reduce the debate on secularism to the question of the headscarf (to "a bit of cloth," as some people said, trying to keep its role in proportion) or to the desire to broaden the definition of secularism in its relation to various religions, and not simply Islam (a desire expressed by the Stasi commission in its report[2]), it is nonetheless the headscarf that provided the cement for this debate, not without triggering collective passions and even a certain "political hysteria."[3] Instead of being open and involving several voices, this monotone and consensual debate, which became more heated as the "contagion"[4] spread, once again confirmed social cohesion and the republican spirit by celebrating secularism and the equality of the sexes. It nonetheless witnessed the encounter between the republic and Islam, an encounter in which the feminine subject was central "amid violence, uncertainties, and strategies of freedom."

In contrast to the conceptualization of the public sphere proposed by Jürgen Habermas, which privileges rational discussion, the struggle over the veil (not only in France but also in Turkey, where discussion has been equally passionate for the past two decades), reveals the "emotional" terrain and the role of the passional in the public debate. The communication of images and information through the media in contemporary societies certainly amplifies their sensorial and emotional aspect. It is under the impact of shocks, sensations, and scandals that the public acts and constructs itself. The veil has a visual force that suddenly appears in the public space and in the collective imagination. But why is it so disturbing? The answer may seem obvious, but shouldn't we question this obviousness itself? The narrative that it presupposes is an integral part of the passional dispute. It is by studying the nature of the passions at work in this conflict and the discord that underlies it that we can better understand what the veil reveals, in an emblematic way, not only about the women who wear it but also about those who oppose it. The debate has in fact confirmed the inscription of the Islamic veil in a strictly French context, and as a French question, by bringing its defenders and its adversaries together and connecting the veil with the historical and cultural experience of France.[5] The public debate attests to this disturbing proximity, to this difficulty in sharing a single public space while at the same time displaying religious and even cultural difference.

Women, Islam, and feminism

The veil marks a turning point in public perceptions of the phenomenon of immigration. The notion of the immigrant—defined in the 1960s as a social category initially composed of workers, and then of *beurs* (children of North African immigrants)[6], and thus always embodied by the masculine gender—changes with the appearance of the feminine gender and the identification of the phenomenon of immigration with Islam. Paradoxically, the headscarf affair has led to the "feminization" of the perception of the Muslim population, and also, correspondingly, of the representation of the republic. The encounter between the republic and Islam, particularly with regard to the Islamic veil, has put the question of women at the center of the definition of social values. Thus the values of secularism, defined primarily in juridical and political terms, are being redefined in the light of the question of women.[7]

French feminism, which used to advocate the values of freedom and the equality of the sexes, includes the values of secularism in its criticism of the Islamic veil. Thus it gains new energy and a new start by advocating these republican and secular values of citizenship and denouncing patriarchal *communautarisme* and religious fundamentalism. Thus we can speak of a convergence, an overlapping, between secular feminism and republicanism. Republican citizenship now overtly and distinctly includes women and women's rights, as is shown by the French president's speech given on the occasion of the passage of the law forbidding the veil. Women's efforts on behalf of this law, especially the public letter signed by famous women and published in the magazine *Elle*, show this consensual convergence. What ambiguities are involved in such a convergence, in particular from the point of view of feminist criticism? Isn't the fact that this letter was addressed to the president of the republic a recognition of patriarchal power and especially its incarnation in a man? Doesn't publishing it in a women's fashion magazine run counter to feminist criticisms of the subjection of women's bodies to the aesthetic criteria of the market and even its commercialization? This debate has in fact encouraged a certain kind of state feminism to step forward and speak in the name of republican secular women, thus establishing boundaries and cleavages with Muslim women. These women turn against the original ideal of the feminist movement that spoke in the name of all women, independently of differences among them, whether these differences were ethnic, race, class, or religious in nature. It is in contrast to the Other, the veiled woman defined by her subjection to Muslim men and her community, that secular feminism has sought to distinguish itself, to endow itself with a new emancipatory, if not civilizing, mission (thereby encouraging new figures of North African, emancipated women to speak out).

We can conclude first of all that the phenomenon of the veil cannot be understood without taking into account the intersubjective and intercultural dimensions that underlie power relationships between the genders. In other words, the veil crystallizes power relationships not only between men and women but also between women. On the other hand, it is not having access to modernity that differentiates these women but rather their cultural orientation. The veil is troublesome mainly because it is entering the spaces of modernity. But it is when the various social spaces are invested by actors with different cultural orientations who enter into conflict for control over these spaces that an intercultural and intersubjective political space emerges. The veil crystallizes these conflicts on the very personal level of the body and raises the question of sharing and conflictual communication, while at the same time referring to a more historical and global temporality, to intercultural and even civilizational difference, in the definitions of the female subject, of the relations between genders, and of the distinction between the private and the public domains.

The conflict of temporalities

It could be objected that this analysis attributes a kind of unity to the veil. We must in fact not ignore or underestimate the diversity covered by the veil, the differences between the women who wear it, the multiplicity of motivations that underlie it, and the social dynamics that cause it to be transformed. But here I would like to draw attention, especially in the pluralist context in which the veil is not imposed but chosen, to the choreography of the conflict, in other words, to the borderlines, the intersections, the clash between religious Muslims and secular feminists, and not limit myself solely to the internal topography of Islam and the veil. My approach follows, in a way, that of the veiled women who are familiar with modernity and in dialogue with it. This process requires an interpretation in terms of relationships at close quarters, conflictual interactions, mutual inspection; an interpretation of the veil in an ambivalent relation to modernity but also an interpretation of modernity that is reversed and decentered in the mirror of the veil. The veil and modernity are connected with each other in terms of the mutual exclusiveness and their relationship, which is far from symmetrical and refers to several historical temporalities—to the present time, while also awakening the long-term memory.

In the statement that it makes, the veil concentrates several historical temporalities. Rather than presuppose a historical continuity, it would no doubt be better to recall that after the historic break represented by the process of unveiling, today we are coming back to the process of reveiling. Colonization, and also voluntary Westernization or even globalization have imposed, in a hegemonic way, an equation between the West's cultural values and modernity that has had an impact on the social practices, institutional foundations, and collective imaginations of Muslim countries.

All through the twentieth century, the question of women has been a subject of controversy at the heart of this process of Westernization: it has been through the place of women in Muslim society that the borderlines between cultural identity and "Western civilization" have been debated. The place of women in public life, their bodily visibility, and their access to citizenship have become major issues for reformers and conservatives in all the Muslim countries, beginning with Turkey and Iran but also including the countries of North Africa. The unveiling of women, their emancipation from the Muslim religion, and their participation in social life, have thus been defined as a priori conditions for national progress. The Muslim woman has been, from the outset, a pillar of progress and national enlightenment. Thus the veil has been rejected by modernizing reformers in Muslim countries as a sign of women's enslavement but also as an obstacle to national progress. Its present return awakens this memory of the past and reproduces the fracture between Muslim women who have won their individual freedom by cutting their ties with religion and those who are re-adapting religion. The memory of the past is inscribed in present conflicts, in the uses that women make of their bodies. The relation to the body becomes the decisive element in the social fracture that separates women from one another, just as it separates cultures.

The reversal of the stigma

The role of the body in intersubjective and intercultural conflicts is shown particularly with regard to the Islamic stigma and its reversal. The language of sociology commonly uses the term *stigmatization* in the figurative sense, in order to designate the exclusion of part of the population that is not recognized or humiliated by social discriminations, verbal harassments, or cultural prejudices. But I would like to come back to the initial meaning of the term, to its more direct relation to the body, and to the social information about the individual that it conveys. Erving Goffman reminds us that the notion of "stigma" has lost its original sense; in Greek, it meant the marks inscribed on the body with a knife or red-hot iron to designate an individual who had committed some heinous offense and who had to be shunned in public places. The term *stigma* thus designates one or more bodily signs providing "social information" about the individual, an attribute that casts deep discredit on him (for example, the shaved heads of women "collaborators" after the Second World War).[8] By using the notion of "stigma," I seek to display the bodily domain as a direct mediation of the production of difference—but a difference that is not desired and disqualifies the individual in the public space.

The Islamic veil is a bodily sign; not hereditary, like the color of one's skin, not permanent, like a scar left by a knife, it is a sign that has been adopted, whether under constraint or not. Nor is it quite like a tattoo or a body-piercing, which are signs of the youth culture. Girls' resistance to taking off their veils, the subversive strategies they have invented by wearing hats or wigs as parodic signs—like some Turkish women university students—show very clearly the character of the veil. It concerns their private persons, while at the same time referring to the collective subject, that is, to Islam. It is a religious sign that is incorporated personally and communicated socially. Speaking of an Islamic stigma is a way of making it possible to reflect not only on what belongs to the domain of the person, by way of the body, but also to the interpersonal and public domain, because the stigma implies perception and thus is not separate from the hegemony of modernity in the hierarchization of aesthetic and ethical values.

As Goffman suggests, it is a language of communication, of relationships, that we have to understand, and not simply a language of attributes. It is not the attribute in itself, as a thing like the veil, but rather the cultural quality that it conveys that determines the perception of the stigma. By reflecting on the problem of deviancy, Goffman thus makes a distinction between the "stigmatized" and the "normal" and contrasts the symbols of prestige with those of stigmatization. The notion of stigma concerns the domain of the body as much as it does the cognitive and interrelational domain. As we have seen, modernity made the veil a stigmatizing symbol, a symbol of the enslavement of women that discredited the person and the social group that adopted it. Today, the return of the Islamic veil signifies the adoption—voluntary or imposed, depending on the case—of a sign of "stigma" on the part of women who wear it while at the same time seeking to reverse the meaning of that sign, to turn it into a sign of "prestige." The Islamist trend situates itself in a similar logic by seeking, through the production of religious difference and its exacerbation through "ostentatious" signs, to acquire public visibility and to seize symbolic as well as political power.

Behind these "ostentatious" signs or religious visibility looms the desire to invert their value and make them symbolize a distinct prestige and power in accord with a process that is already proceeding in Iran and Turkey by paths and trajectories that are very different and even opposed. While in Iran the revolution made the Islamic veil a symbol of power imposed from above, in Turkey the veil, which is prohibited in the institutional sphere of public life, acquires the sense of a protest from below. In Iran, in the postrevolutionary period, it was being "incompletely veiled" that took on the meaning of a protest,[9] whereas in Turkey advocates of the Islamic veil seek to give it legitimacy through the established political power but also through the aesthetic strategies of fashion in order to gain social prestige.

In other terms, we have to adjust our perception of the veil and the women who wear it and who seek, not without peril, to transform its symbolic meaning. If the recognition of the personal and bodily aspect of the veil is a problem, that is because it presupposes the recognition, at least in a context of political pluralism, of the existence of a feminine agency, of personal decisions made by women. Every debate on the veil encounters this blind spot: every criticism of the veil is based on a denial of the Muslim woman's individual agency and consequently on the denunciation of the Muslim man, the masculine entourage, Islamic governments, or community pressures. The veil thus appears as the instrument of a double subjection of women, by religion on the one hand, and by masculine power on the other. Although this criticism is not false, it is nonetheless incomplete. Today, the veil depends, at least among some Muslim women, on an individual religious choice, which is at the same time situated in the Islamist movement, that is, in the collective assertion of a conflictual difference from the secular values of egalitarian liberalism. The veil signifies the emergence of the female actor in the city and in the Islamist movement. We can even go so far as to say that what distinguishes contemporary Islamist movements from earlier fundamentalisms is the emergence within them of the feminine subject but with all the ambivalence that veiled women maintain with regard to the notion of the subject and freedom of action.

Religious action constitutes a blind spot in the public debate because the cognitive system and the *doxa* of modernity do not recognize any place for the religious. For the narrative of modernity, the religious actor is considered "premodern" or even, in the case of Islam, "antimodern"; he or she is doomed to disappear from the public space as the historical process of secularization proceeds. Modern society defines citizenship, that is equality of access to the public space, to political agency and to the right to speak by the secular condition. The veiled woman who demands to be present in the public space challenges, without intending to, the cognitive and implicit schemas of modernity. The question of women is at the heart of this dispute because the modernity of the present time is constructed with reference to the equality of the sexes. In other words, it is the relations between the sexes, but also between persons of the same sex, that are now agitating modern societies. That is why this social debate is becoming a quarrel between women and even a quarrel about women and ways of defining feminism.

Another use of the body

The veil serves as an amplifier for this quarrel through a nonverbal kind of communication: it stages another use of the body than that of the "liberated" woman. The modern veil displays women at the same time that it conceals them. Although it incorporates the precepts of the Islamic religion, the social grammar of the prohibitions bearing on seeing and on the body, it also corresponds to the stakes involved in adornments, effects of "stylization." Georg Simmel showed how stylizing is a "calming response to the exaggerated subjectivism of the time, a "retreat," the individual's reserve, a manifestation of modesty and discretion."[10] Adornment concerns the relations between the particular and the general, between the subjective and the intersubjective. It distinguishes and even creates distance insofar as it causes the person to *enter* into a form shared by others. The modern adornment of the veil is situated in this "in-between": it is both "modern and Muslim." It is situated halfway between proximity to the secular woman emancipated from religion and alterity with respect to the traditional Muslim woman.

We have to recall that with the feminism of the 1970s, the grammar of women's liberation was defined by the body. The female body sought to free itself from the chains of biological difference (by obtaining the right to abortion and contraception), from submission to male desire, and from sexual violence, and it took its revenge by making publicly visible this body and sexuality in quest of freedom. Feminism not only changed women's relation to men but also women's relation to their own bodies. We can also interpret this process as an entrance of the woman's body into the spiral of an accelerated secularization. A culture of "care for the self," in which one "gives oneself pleasure" and "is concerned with one's body" shows, moreover, how the body becomes the site of the cult not only of freedom but also of neoliberalism (which probably explains as well the recent alliance between some feminists and the magazine *Elle*).

Confronted by the Western woman's body, which is considered as a symbol of aesthetic prestige and freedom and has become an object of idolatry, the Islamic body, by obeying precepts of a divine order, religious rituals, and the supervision of pleasures (*nefs*), introduces an element of invisibility and abstraction into the female body. The risk for women is that they might succeed in abstracting themselves from the social body in limiting their physical presence in the public space. Religious action involves uncertainties about freedoms: between freedom of action and religious submission, the distance is not great. The criticism of the subjection of the body by recalling the notion of the beyond can lead to a new and dialogic reflection on the paths of liberty.

In the act of wearing the veil, we can discern a criticism of the extreme logic of the emancipation of women that is based on the body alone. Without being completely in control of the meaning of this act, covering herself is, for the veiled woman, a way of saving herself from the generalized secularization that unites the diverse domains of life, from procreation to aesthetics, and causes them to enter an alarming spiral of uninterrupted change and innovation. In other words, the Enlightenment project constantly shifts the borderlines between nature and culture and carries out the gradual transfer of the different domains of nature into the register of a choice that is cultural and thus individual by transforming the woman's body into a marker of this change. In the past, contraception and abortion (and today, genetic engineering) moved reproduction into the universe of personal choice and thus displaced the cursor form the natural domain toward the cultural. This process undeniably means greater personal freedom to choose one's own life, but it also means increased obedience to the logic of the market. Above all, it institutes a major challenge to the moral and ethical order. The revival of religion in the contemporary world indicates that the achievements of ultra-modernity are being challenged. Religion in general and the act of wearing the veil in particular recall the submission of the person to other values; thus they privilege a certain dose of humility over the secular, all-powerful will of the modern subject. But once again, as a marker of the values of modesty or pride, of submission or emancipation, it is the woman's body that is at the heart of the power relationships and the woman question. The female subject, veiled or not, challenges the modern subject that seeks itself in the uncertainties of the strategies of freedom.

CHAPTER 12

Identifying Europe: Alterizing Turkey?

Climbing into a taxi at the Marseille train station, I noticed a little blue amulet against the "evil eye" suspended from rear-view mirror. This amulet looked more like the Turkish ones that one finds in all the taxis in Istanbul than like the North African version of the same thing. I asked the taxi driver about it, and it turned out that he was not, in fact, North African but Armenian. He had bought the amulet in Greece. Then he asked me about my "slight accent." I replied that I was Turkish.

We fell silent, and I tried to restart the conversation by asking him what he thought about Turkey's candidacy for admission to the European Union. It was the middle of November, 2004, when the debate about this issue was extremely heated in France. His reply was as brief as it was categorical. He was against admitting Turkey, because in his view a Muslim country had no place in Europe, even if he felt no hostility toward immigrants. I tried again by emphasizing the pacifying dimension of the European project, which could improve relations between Christians and Muslims, and encourage Turks to come to terms with their own past and recognize the Armenian genocide. Far from being convinced, he told me that "all the wars were religious wars." Our conversation ended when we arrived at our destination, but it remained in my memory—as much for the arguments we had exchanged as for the self-examination it had involved. I was not insensitive to the fact that an Armenian from eastern Turkey had chosen to buy his good-luck charm in Greece. As I have repeatedly noticed, Turks are often reminded of their duty of remembrance with regard to the Armenians by some object or place during a personal exchange. As I have witnessed myself, in personal life experiences, in face-to-face conversations, Turks are often called upon to waken from their amnesia with regard to the Armenian past. I could not help thinking that beyond differences in religion, we were connected by a common culture that allowed us to feel a familiarity that members of the same religion do not necessarily share. The belief that one can protect oneself against the evil eye was one example among many others. To this superstition we could add common tastes in food and the same sense of hospitality. In cultural areas like the Mediterranean or the Orient, we find common points, a tacit agreement despite religious differences. Culture and religion do not always coincide. It is perhaps precisely this difficulty in establishing the separation and recognizing the difference between the two that has today become a major issue for humanity and for Europe in particular.

From opinions to public opinion

The interest anthropologists and sociologists take in conversations with taxi drivers probably proceeds from the fact that the latter show the interface between the personal and the public. The conversation takes place in a private means of transportation, in the closed space of the taxi, but between two people foreign to one another. It is an accidental meeting, the product of urban anonymity, but it is also a form of "privatized" encounter that is not overheard by the general public. In a taxi, we are moving not only through the city but also through information, rumors, and opinions. A taxi driver's opinion can also be representative of so-called public opinion.

The remarks of my taxi driver in Marseille, even though they were personal and marked by the Armenian memory of genocide and the experience of diaspora, were in harmony with those of a large segment of French public opinion. The correspondence between one person's opinion and public opinion is a complex phenomenon. Social position, subjective memory, and also access to information and public debate play a decisive role in shaping opinions. Each individual enters public opinion through a personal door, a singular history, in order to give form to what might be considered a manifest and collective trait of public opinion.

However, not every opinion constitutes a public opinion. According to the thinkers of the seventeenth century, opinion is only a simple expression of "common sense," the ways and customs prevailing in society, unfounded judgments, or even prejudices. Thus there is a tension between this initial definition of opinion and the one that succeeded it, which elaborated the notion of public opinion. In his reflections on the genealogy of the concept of public opinion, Habermas shows how the latter evolved in relation to the use of reason and against the prejudices of opinions. In France, the opposition between opinion and truth, judgment and reason, opinion and criticism, was long very clear cut. It was with the physiocrats that the notion of an "enlightened public" first appeared, a public that was constituted through critical discussion in the public sphere.[1] Thus starting in the eighteenth century, public opinion and the use of critical reason began to converge. But these two notions were not always conceived of as an inseparable couple. For Rousseau, for example, the "general will" was based on the consensus of people's hearts rather than on that of arguments; by avoiding "thorny discussions," society is better governed, thanks to laws that correspond to the simplicity of common ways and customs.[2] In Habermas's definition of the public sphere as the ideal type of democracy, public debate is the place where prejudices and opinions are the object of critical and discursive communication. An opinion transformed by the use of reason is no longer a simple opinion, in the sense of a simple inclination, but rather a private reflection on public affairs and their discussion in public.

Today, the more populist interpretation of the notion of public opinion pays little attention to the idea of an enlightened public, which it sees as having elitist connotations. Thus we are witnessing a kind of sacralization of public opinion as a new, positive figure of the collectivity. For instance, it is claimed, on the basis of polls and percentages, that the majority of the French people is hostile to the Turkish candidacy for admission to the EU.[3] Public opinion thus becomes an indisputable given that cannot be subjected to critical debate.

The debate over Turkey illustrates a new stage in the construction of Europe, showing that the latter is no longer the domain of political decision-makers and bureaucrats in Brussels, and that it is for the people to declare its opinion, whether through polls or through referenda, a consultation that thus enters into the political game. In a way, here the idea of popular sovereignty and the truth-principle of the modern nation-state are both applied to the European project. The political development that leads to considering it necessary to consult "the people," and thus to organize a referendum on opening negotiations with Turkey, is one example of this. Popular sovereignty and its corollary, public opinion, tend to become an unavoidable collective persona regarding the democratic aspirations of the European project. But then it would be appropriate to look into the nature of this democratic aspiration.

The celebration of the role of public opinion in democracy is not new, any more than it concerns the debate over Turkey alone. But as Pierre Rosanvallon has shown, in contemporary democratic societies, public opinion is changing in register. Formerly a mode of political opposition, the spontaneous voice of civil society, it is now becoming an expression of cultural identity.[4] What is involved is a new consecration of public opinion: the social recognition and popularity of polls correspond to the desire to break with democratic abstraction and restore a voice and a face to the people. Thus formulas of the type "the French think that..." are ways of staging this, and "it is almost always a question of a society understood as a person."[5] According to Rosanvallon, in seeking to delimit and define the morale, the moods, expectations, or demands of the people, we are witnessing a kind of return to the old nineteenth-century theory of the psychology of peoples or nations. And when public opinion, which is indispensable to the life of democracy, becomes the consecration of a new figure of the "people-opinion," there is a temptation to drift toward an "essentialist democracy": this kind of personification of the collectivity derives identity from a double movement of concealing society's internal divisions and exacerbating the differences with what is external or foreign to it."[6] The permanent specter of an internal or external enemy, the denunciation of anything that can threaten the people's identity, encourage in turn, as Rosanvallon points out, the rise of a populist politics such as that pursued by the *Front National* in France.[7]

Europe, an identity or a project?

The terms of the public debate on the compatibility of Turkey's joining Europe and the European project, which began before the opening of negotiations with Turkey, namely October 3, 2005, and has continued to grow in importance in French public opinion, call for reflection on the nature of this debate and its connection with cultural identity. It is the discussions of Turkey's candidacy that have shown how difficult the relations between identity and alterity are: the possible presence of Turkey within the EU has provoked, at least in France, a discussion of what the identity of Europe is or should be.

The debate about Turkey has become a debate about identity in which the opponents of Turkey's admission seek to define the difference or alterity between two worlds by reference to geographical borders, religion, the Armenian question, the status of women, or cultural manners. It has established a repertory of themes that help increase the distance separating Turkey from Europe: geographical borders (Iran, Iraq) and cultural borders, the Islamist specter, the size of the population—all these themes strengthen reluctance and the imaginary of fear. We are seeing a dynamics of distancing from Turkey that I would describe as the desire to "alterize" Turkey. On the one hand, this debate has aroused the expression of feelings and prejudices proceeding from a sedimented historical memory. Opinions that are thought to be natural, constituting a kind of *doxa*, form a "primordial" opinion that has hardly changed in its psycho-sociological structure.[8] But it is onto the background of this sedimented historical memory and its psycho-sociological structure, which indicate a "classical" alterity based on old stereotypes, that a new repertory of arguments weighing on the collective imaginary has been grafted.

Today, the discussion is caught up in the spiral of a production of Turkish alterity that goes so far as to depict the entry of Turkey into the EU as a threat and the fulfillment of the wishes of Europe's enemies.[9] This does not mean that no criticism worthy of the name is being conducted. Some politicians and intellectuals, of all persuasions, are demanding a more reasoned debate on the arguments in favor of the Turkish candidacy, precisely in order to move beyond identity-related and civilizational fixations. But these voices are in the minority. On the whole, the debate is monotone (even though it bears on different themes). The consequence is a mobilization of feelings and a plethora of negative arguments leading to the formation of a public opinion that is resistant or even hostile to the idea of Turkey's inclusion.

The admission of Turkey into the EU constitutes a special case for the European project, and it is very revealing that its candidacy has elicited a debate, perhaps the first of its kind, on the definition of Europe. But the possibility of a rapprochement between Turkey and Europe seems to touch on something hidden, implicit, emotional, or even irrational in the way the French in particular define their identity. It can also be maintained that in our democracies indifferent to alterity we need an Other to avert a lack of identity and mobilize collective energies. The fact that Turkey has become the key site of difference and alterity that allows us to recall a common heritage, a homogeneous basis, might seem to some people normal and even desirable. But no one can be unaware that the debate about this country tests Europe's ability to cope with alterity, as well as its ability to construct democracy and peace. The two aspects are connected, because it is in and through the constitution of the public space that European democracies conceive of their relation to the Other, to the foreign, to immigration, and also all the forms of difference undergone or demanded. There is a fundamental link between the public space and the relation to alterity; the debate about cultural identity plays on the feeling of fear and makes this relation difficult to conceive of in inclusive and democratic terms.

Paradoxically, the "alterization" of Turkey occurred when the latter approached Europe and showed its political determination to begin a process of social transformation in conformity with the European democratic perspective.[10] In other words, the debate began precisely when Turkey became a credible candidate, thus positioning itself as an interlocutor and possible partner of Europe.

Turkey is in fact showing signs of moving beyond alterity, delays, and fixations related to cultural identity that are of a governmental, national, or religious nature. Contrary to what Turko-skeptics claim, the legislative reforms made to bring the Turkish legal system into conformity with the Copenhagen criteria have been more than "cosmetic"; they have been accompanied by a genuine social mobilization (*seferberlik*). Far from being reducible to laws approved by the parliament without the involvement of Turkish society, these transformations have been brought about by human rights movements and the activities of civic associations, business, and intellectuals, as well as politicians and especially the government. For example, without a heated public debate on the Kurdish question, it would not have been possible for parliament to abolish capital punishment while Abdullah Öcalan, the leader of the PKK, was in prison. Such an advance can be envisaged only within the framework of a critique of assimilating nationalism. Along the same lines, making "honor killings" punishable by law, a step supported by Turkish feminist organizations, has contributed to the in-depth democratization of Turkish society and served as a consensual ideal. The European project has been taken over by the domestic project and shared by a large number of actors.

I do not seek to present Turkey as a country without problems but rather to show how the European perspective makes it possible to move beyond them. In this sense, Europeanness is nothing other than a society's capacity for self-criticism, to detect its own problems, name them, and make them a public issue in order to propose legislative solutions to them in the framework of a government of laws. It is in this sense that we see Europeanization at work in Turkey. In the age of globalization, the project of Europe supports the social action that is in danger of disappearing between neoliberalism and ultra-conservatism.

Not recognizing the Europeanness of Turkey, "alterizing" it, orientalizing, Islamizing, or even barbarizing it, amounts to defining Europe as an identity and not as a project. It has been possible to envisage Turkey's candidacy only because of the abandonment of the purity of an identity defined in nationalist or religious terms. On the other hand, the presence of Turkey in Europe challenges and disturbs the tacit equation of European identity with the Judeo-Christian heritage. It requires a redefinition of the European project that separates the cultural from the religious and moves beyond obsessions and identity-related passions.

If we define Europeanness as a project and not as a given identity, we are putting the emphasis on the process and on the democratic capacity for continually facing up to the question of alterity. It is a question of transcending identity-related borderlines between Islam and the West, between Turkey and Europe. Thus the Armenian genocide must have its place in this process of "dismantling" notions of identity. This requires critical analysis of Turkish public opinion, of prejudices, buried convictions, and historical sedimentations—in short, intellectual work and the construction of an enlightened public.

To return to the initial question concerning the relation between public opinion and an enlightened public, I would like to point out the opposition between the necessarily interwoven notions of public opinion and secrecy—a derived form of the opposition between inside and outside.[11] By definition, secrecy delimits a domain exterior to public opinion; once institutionalized, every public space reproduces new secret spaces in order to be able to continue to practice politics. The latter requires the existence of secret places for debate organized by intellectuals and interest groups. These places are an indispensable precondition for public debate. Thus taboos and prejudices have to be questioned and certain reforms have to be made in limited group—if one is to have any chance of carrying out these reforms. The European project can move forward and respond to the challenge of cultural identity only if it restores the limits of public opinion by means of preliminary enlightened discussions.

CHAPTER 13

Giving Up European "Purity"

When the question of "Islam" and "the West" is raised, it is usually approached in terms of geographic or civilizational difference and not in terms of proximity. From a historical point of view, however, we know that at least during the colonial episode the Muslim world was marked by a modernization that was as strong as it was deliberate, and we know how much it has been affected today by globalization. The proximity of the two cultures is further accentuated by migrations, both ancient and recent. The imprint left by these developments is certainly not symmetrical. Muslims took the West as their model of development, not the other way around. The great values of Western modernity, such as secularism and the equality of the sexes, have imbued the social imagination, resulting in the establishment of institutions and profound changes in individual practices, particularly in Turkey but also elsewhere in the Muslim world. That is, it is not enough to speak of some "delay" or "deficit" of modernity in describing the Muslim world. On the contrary, an excess of modernity can sometimes be noted, as in the case of secularism in Turkey, where the Jacobin model, associated with the power of the army, has resulted in a "muscular" or even authoritarian secularism. We can also cite the victories won in the area of women's rights, which in Turkey as in Muslim countries as a whole, have often posed less of a problem than respect for "human rights."

This modernity, understood as a project and as a social imagination, has led in Muslim countries to a kind of "detraditionalization" much more extensive than in European countries. What has changed over the past two decades is precisely Muslims' relationship to modernity. It is here that we encounter the term *Islamism,* meaning a rejection of assimilation and a critique of the mimetic relation to the West—"Westernization" and "modernization" having been considered for centuries synonymous. Today, the meaning of this Islamist movement must be reinterpreted as an attempt to reappropriate this relation to modernity. This is the common point underlying the search for a generic appellation, "Islamism" or "Islamic movement," despite the diverse forms taken by this phenomenon—the Iranian revolution, the terrorism of September 11, Turkish parliamentary democracy, the development of individualist practices, etc. This is to suggest the existence of a new value assigned to Islam at the heart of Muslims' quest for identity itself, in spite of the fact that they are already operating in full modernity, whether through immigration, secular education, scientific training, or political practice.

In this sense, Islam no longer refers to populations attached to a territory, a place, and traditions. Scholars have clearly shown the extent to which deracination can lead to terrorist activity or become a source of alienation. Here we are far from the old equation of modernity and mobility: those who had freed themselves from their customs, left their lands, and become urban or even cosmopolitan, used to be called "modern." Although today more emphasis is put on the "local," this term was formerly used primarily, in contrast to "global," to refer to a group that had remained attached to its traditions and was for that reason considered outside modernity. But these days Muslims are engaged in a process of geographical and cultural mobility that is well illustrated by their situation in Europe. For them, Islam no longer means territorial attachment but rather an intellectual construction that is deliberately, individually, and collectively chosen.

The victory of the Justice and Development Party (AKP) in the general elections of Novmber 3, 2002, testifies to the possibility of change in Islamists' mind-set. This is still an ongoing process, which makes its labeling difficult. The very name given to this political group raises many questions: does it refer to a moderate Islam, Muslim democrats, or conservative Islam? The AKP won the elections by moving toward the center, that is, toward mainstream politics, rather than by radicalizing its discourse. Furthermore, it was under its leadership that Turkey began to struggle for admission to the EU. And if Turks long believed they could forget and make Europeans forget that they were part of the Muslim world—that is why they committed themselves so fully to secularism—, they are, by an irony of history, Muslims who declare themselves pro-European. This two-way perspective and this paradox cannot be ignored. Will Europe be able to create a space for these democratic, reformist Muslims? This is a crucial question for Europe as well, and true change in the relations between Islam and Europe depends on the answer: if a short time ago Muslims were still looking toward the West, now the West must turn toward Muslims and try to discern their differences.

Doing away with the equation "The West = civilization"

To speak of public space is to speak both of opening up and of connecting with the Other. The public space thus defines the borderlines between those who are included and those who excluded, for there is no "opening up" without an establishment of limits. The second characteristic of the public space is the kind of neutrality that is called secularism, and it is particularly characteristic of the French model. To be part of this space and have access to the debate, one has to accept the rules governing this neutral space, setting aside religious differences. Finally, there is no public space without a private space. To understand contemporary Islam is thus to inquire more deeply into its relations with the public space and with Europe. Today, Islam is emerging in the public space, and its visibility disturbs people. The Islamic headscarf, the demand that mosques be constructed, halal meat, or the debate over the calendar—everything that has to do with everyday life is important in the definition of the Muslim subject and the latter's recently acquired visibility in European public spaces.

Today Islam is not reducible to an ideology: the notion of Islamism does not suffice to define it if this notion is taken to designate a rigid structure controlled by militants. There is an Islamic social imagination. In Europe, an Islam that is increasingly internalized seems to be developing in practices. These behaviors—which are already flourishing in spaces of modernity such as universities, in political life, and in urban milieus—seem to me to reflect an appropriation of modernity and a criticism of it. They convey first of all a resistance to the liberal definition of the subject in the sense that they contain a reminder of the boundaries of modesty and chastity. That is why every public manifestation of Islam also constitutes a reminder of the private, the forbidden, the secret, the sacred. Thus the headscarf, for instance, constitutes a way of appealing, in public, to private life. The major cultural criticism bears on the equation of the West with "civilization."

The question of the headscarf is central for understanding contemporary Islam. Rather than being a political act, the headscarf is part of a history of manners and of the way in which Muslim subjects define themselves within modernity. The question of women crystallizes this ambivalence. Far from being merely an epiphenomenon of a broader activism, this question is at the heart of the debate because it refers to a more cultural dimension, to a production of new norms. Women in fact have left the traditional space: they have gained a foothold in public life, in schools, in the parliament, and in the media. Unlike their counterparts in earlier generations, women who wear the headscarf today are crossing the threshold of tradition, moving into the public space, demanding a share of the positions in universities, etc. The question is consequently whether people are ready to redefine and renegotiate the public space's boundaries of inclusion and exclusion. This is the case not only in France and other European countries but also in Turkey, a country with a Muslim majority.

Rethinking the foundations of the European public space

The question of women is emblematic: it reveals the limits of the European secular public space at the same time that it is located at the heart of the dynamics of Islamist movements. The difficulty for Muslims thus consists in preserving a difference within the very heart of modernity, in making contraries coexist: affirming a difference without destroying modernity or identifying themselves with modernity without renouncing Islam, as secular Turks do. If in Europe Muslims have to recognize their everyday experiences of secular ways of life, and they are beginning to do that, Europe also has to reflect critically on its own definitions of modernity and its hegemonic cultural prerequisites.

Shouldn't Europe ask itself where it stands with regard to civilization, whether its civilizing mission might be coming to an end? ("Civilization" being understood less in the sense given it by Samuel Huntington than in the one given it by the sociologist Norbert Elias: "a sense of the superiority of Western manners"[1]). In the past, Muslims have adopted this definition as their own without quite realizing what they were doing, undertaking to rid themselves of their cultural particularities, including Islam and its traditions and even their ways of life, in order to move gradually nearer to this civilization considered universal and positivist. This logic of assimilation now seems outdated for Muslims, just as the notion of a civilizing mission is outdated for Europeans. In their place is emerging the notion of a distinction and a separation of civilizations (a conflictual notion if ever there was one), defended in particular by proponents of the thesis of the "clash of civilizations."

What is peculiar to Europe and the West is nonetheless this capacity to create a relation to the Other, to the foreign, a capacity that is also called democracy. The closure of the European space is not without a certain resemblance to fundamentalist Islam: what meaning could be assigned to a Europe that claimed to be "pure," to have an almost essentialist identity? To recognize Islam within the European public space is no doubt to give up the new clothes donned by the civilizing mission in the nineteenth century. Don't we have to begin thinking about the foundations of the public space, trying to find a new definition for it? Don't we need to rethink the notion of secularism and the borderlines between public life and private life? If the debate is painful and charged with emotion, that is probably because we have to question European identity and give up its "purity."

Notes

Introduction

1. *Babel*, directed by Alejandro González Iñárritu; written by Guillermo Arriaga; starring Brad Pitt, with Cate Blanchett, Gael García Bernal, and Kôji Yakusho. Released by Paramount Vantage, 2006.
2. A. O. Scott, "Emotions Need No Translation," *New York Times*, October 27, 2006.
3. Samuel P. Huntington, *The Clash of Civilizations and the Remaking of World Order*. New York: Simon and Schuster, 1996, 28.
4. Ibid., 139.
5. Samuel P. Huntington,*Who Are We: The Challenges to America's National Identity*. Simon and Schuster: New York, 2004.
6. Jacques Derrida, *L'Autre Cap*, Éditions de Minuit : Paris, 1991.
7. Claude Lefort, *Essais sur le politique*: XIXe-XXe siècles, Paris : Seuil, 1986.
8. Metin Heper and Şule Toktaş, "Islam, Modernity, and Democracy in Contemporary Turkey : The Case of Recep Tayyip Erdoğan", in *The Muslim World*, Volume 93, Issue 2, pages, 157–185, 14 April 2003.
9. It was said that the author of the poem was the famous Ziya Gökalp. Indeed Gökalp (1876–1924) did write a poem called "Soldier's Prayer." However, the poem was first published in 1913 during the Balkan wars and did not contain the lines that Erdoğan was jailed for reciting.
10. "Protest at Mosque", *The Washington Post*, Tuesday, February 23, 2010. Muslim women staged a protest at a D.C. mosque to demand that mosque leaders remove a seven-foot partititon behind which women pray separately from men.
11. "Women in Mosques, Making Our Case with a Pray-In", by Sarrah Abulughod, www.altmuslimah.com, March 8, 2010.
12. The gathering took place in a castle in western Germany, in the heart of a former industrial region, and was pointedly called the "Anti-Minaret Conference." A common "islamophobia" brought together delegates from the Belgian nationalists Vlaams Belang, Geert Wilder's Dutch Party for Freedom, the Front National of Jean-Marie Le Pen from France, the Pro-Cologne movement from Germany, and others from Sweden, Austria, and Eastern Europe. Charles Hawley, "Following in Switzerland's Footsteps:

International Right-Wingers Gather for EU-Wide Minaret Ban," *Spiegel*, March 26, 2010.

Chapter 2

1. As in the title of Sofia Coppola's film, *Lost in Translation*, January 2004.
2. Clifford Geertz, *Works and Lives: The Anthropologist as Author* (1988). Rpt. Stanford, CA: Stanford UP, 1990.
3. The names to be used for both are problematic. It is difficult to designate Europe as a homogeneous, well-defined entity with fixed borders. Similarly, Islam is not a homogeneous entity, either. This book seeks to offer an analytical way of moving beyond these simplifications. The goal is to understand how these names are shaped by an intersubjective and intercultural process.
4. Paul Ricoeur, *La Mémoire, l'Histoire, l'Oubli*. Paris: Seuil, 2000, 161–162. I thank Olivier Abel for having drawn my attention to this approach to contemporaneity.
5. Dipesh Chakrabarty, *Provincializing Europe: Postcolonial Thought and Historical Difference*. Princeton NJ: Princeton UP, 2000.
6. Edgar Morin shows how European historiography has externalized Turkey even though it was a European empire. Thus in the famous Battle of Kosovo (1389), where the Ottomans defeated the Serbs, there were Christians in the Ottoman army and Muslims in the Serb army. (Edgar Morin, « Le test européen. » *Le Journal du Dimanche*, October 10, 2004.)
7. Schmuel N. Eisenstadt and Wolfgang Schlüchter, "Introduction: Paths to Early Modernities. A Comparative View, *Daedalus* 127 (3) (1998), 6.
8. Michael Ignatieff, *Kaboul-Sarajevo. Les Nouvelles frontières de l'empire*. Paris: Seuil, 2002.
9. A book by Ivo Andric, winner of the Nobel Prize for literature in 1961, *The Bridge on the Drina* (Chicago: University of Chicago Press, 1977), provides a good explanation of the complexity of Bosnian identity.
10. Predrag Matvejevic, "Ce pont entre Orient et Occident. In *Stari most. Le vieux pont de Mostar*, ed. G. Péqueux and Y. Le Corre. Paris: Gallimard, 2002.
11. Ibid., 28.
12. Interview with Gilles Péqueux, the engineer in charge of the design, coordination, and supervision of the studies for the reconstruction of the bridge at Mostar, on the occasion of the *Journée du Courrier des Balkans*, March 1, 2003.
13. The Appeals Division of the International Criminal Court for ex-Yugoslavia definitively confirmed, on April 19, 2004, that the massacre of Bosnian Muslims at Srebrenica in 1995 constituted a genocide. Ten years later, on June 11, 2005, the date of the massacre of 8,000 Muslim men and boys by Serb forces was commemorated as the worst organized mas-

sacre in Europe since the Second World War.
14. M. Ignatieff, op. cit., 27.
15. See Daniel Liebeskind's autobiography, *Breaking Ground: An Immigrant's Journey from Poland to Ground Zero*. New York: Riverhead, 2005.
16. The original statue was officially presented to the United States on July 4, 1884, in Paris. The Statue of Liberty represents a woman draped in a toga and holding a torch in her right hand. On the tablets she holds in her left hand are written, in Roman numerals, "July 4, 1776." At her feet lie the broken chains of slavery.
17. Diana West, "A mosque to mock 9/11's victims and families," *Washington Examiner*, May 16, 2010.
18. Clyde Haberman, "Near Ground Zero, the Sacred and the Profane," *The New York Times*, May 27, 2010.
19. The *Lieux de mémoire* project directed by Pierre Nora (Paris: Gallimard, 1994–1997) sought to grasp historical places as historical objects to be analyzed in order to understand the national construction of memory. But globalization is transforming the relation between places and memory.
20. Paul Ricoeur, *La Mémoire, l'Histoire, l'Oubli.*, op cit.; Régine Robin, *La Mémoire saturée*, Paris: Stock, 2003. Cf. also Alexandra Laignel-Lavastine, "Face à l'histoire. La recherche d'une juste mémoire," *Le Monde*, May 22, 2005, 12.
21. I borrow this expression from *Varieties of World Making: Beyond Globalization*, ed. N. Karagiannis and P. Wagner. Liverpool: Liverpool UP, 2006.
22. Title of an article that appeared in the British weekly *The Economist* after the London attacks, July 16–22, 2005, 24.
23. Annelies Moors, "Submission," *Debates on Islam in Europe*, ISIM Review 15 (2005).
24. José Casanova has drawn attention to the growing role of religions in modern life. He shows how religions are "deprivatized"; both Catholicism and Protestantism, in diverse countries such as Spain, Portugal, Brazil, and the United States, no longer limit themselves to the private sphere and invade public life. Cf. José Casanova, *Public Religions in the Modern World*, Chicago: University of Chicago Press, 1994.
25. The publication of the ad for the "Marithé et François Girbeaud" brand of clothing was banned by the Superior Court of Paris on March 10, 2005, deciding in favor of the plaintiff, the Catholic association "Croyances et libertés." Cf. *Le Monde 2* April 2, 2005, 39–40.
26. Monique Canto-Sperber, *Le Bien, la Guerre et la Terreur*. Paris: Plon, 2005, 30.
27. Pierre Vidal-Naquet, *La Démocratie grecque vue d'ailleurs*. Paris: Flammarion, 1996.
28. Paul Berman's book *Terror and Liberalism* (New York: Norton, 2004)

shows the impact of European anti-liberal thought on the mind of contemporary Islamists.
29. For a critique of the over-Islamization of the debates, cf. Dounia Bouzar, *Monsieur Islam n'existe pas: pour une déislamisation des débats*. Paris: Hachette, 2004.
30. Patrick Haenni, "Ils n'en ont pas fini avec l'Orient. De quelques islamisations non islamistes." In *Le Post-islamisme*, special issues of the *Revue des mondes musulmans et de la Méditerranée*, ed. O. Roy and P. Haenni (no. 85–86, 1999).
31. For case studies on the public modalities of Islam in Europe, Turkey, and Iran, see *Islam in Sicht. Der Auftritt von Muslimen im öffentlichen Raum*, ed. N. Göle and L. Amman. Bielefeld: Transcript, 2004. And, more particularly, Simonetta Tabboni's article (p. 326–341), which elaborates the problem of difference and proximity through the notion of the foreigner.
32. For the concept of "different space" (*autre espace*), "heterotopy," cf. Michel Foucault, "Des espaces autres" (1967), in *Dits et écrits, 1980–1988*, ed. D. Defert and F. Ewald. Paris: Gallimard, 1994). On the notions of "counterpublic" (*contre public*) and "subalterns," cf. Michael Warner, *Publics and Counterpublics*. London: Zone, 2002.
33. Hans Joas distinguishes three modes of creativity in human action: the idea of production relates creativity to the world of material objects, the idea of revolution to the social world, and the idea of expression to the subjective world. Cf. Hans Joas, *The Creativity of Action*. Chicago: University of Chicago Press, 1997. (First German edition 1992.)
34. Alain Touraine, *Un nouveau paradigme. Pour comprendre le monde d'aujourd'hui*. Paris: Fayard, 2005.
35. *Time Europe*, "Europe's Identity Crisis." February 28, 2005.
36. I borrow this notion from Serge Moscovici, for whom most social changes are the work of minorities. Cf. *Psychologie des minorités actives*. Paris: PUF, 1996.
37. Niklas Lühmann, *Politique et complexité. Les contributions de la théorie générale des systèmes*. Trans. J. Schmutz. Paris: Editions du Cerf, 1999.
38. Marshall G. S. Hodgson, *The Venture of Islam*, vol. 1, *The Classical Age of Islam*. Chicago: University of Chicago Press, 1974, 81.
39. On the relation between the abolition of the caliphate and the rise of contemporary Islamism, cf. Bobby S. Sayyid, *A Fundamental Fear. Eurocentrism and the Emergence of Islamism*. London and New York: Zed Books, 1997.
40. Sadik J. Al-Azm, "Time out of Joint. Western Dominance, Islamist Terror, and the Arab Imagination." *Boston Review*, October-November 2004.
41. M. Canto-Sperber, *Le Bien, la Guerre et la Terreur*, op. cit., 26.
42. François Georgeon, « L'Empire ottoman et l'Europe aux XIXme siècle. » *Turquie, le 28e étoile? Un défi à relever. Confluences Méditerranée*, no. 52, winter 2004–2005.

43. Tarik Ramadan, a controversial figure of European Islam, seeks to conceptualize the presence of Muslims in Europe. The evolution of the terminology he uses is significant. Cf. Alain Roussillon, *La Pensée islamique contemporaine: acteurs et enjeux*. Paris: Tétraèdre, 2005. Ramadan tries to define the minimal conditions that would allow Muslims to live as a minority in a non-Muslim society without contradicting their membership in the Community of the Faithful. To move beyond the binary division of the world into *dâr al-islam* and *dâr al-harb*, in the early 1990s he proposed speaking of a "space of the pact" or "space of peace" (*dâr al-sulh*), and later introduced the "space of testimony" (*dâr al-shahâda*), where freedom of conscience is protected by constitutions. Cf. Tarik Ramadan, "Les musulmans et la mondialisation." *Pouvoirs*, 104, 2003; by the same author, *Islam. Le face-à-face des civilisations. Quel projet pour quelle modernité?* Lyon: Tawhid, 2001.
44. There is more than one form of anti-Semitism: cf. Michel Wieviorka, *La Tentation antisémite. Haine des Juifs dans la France d'aujourd'hui*. Paris: Robert Laffont, 2005.
45. Jean-Luc Nancy, "L'impossible acte constituant." *Le Monde*, June 29, 2005.

Chapter 3

1. Uğur Kömeçoğlu, "The Publicness and sociabilities of the Ottoman Coffee-house." *The Public*, 12 (2005), 2, 5–22.
2. Claude Lévi-Strauss, *La Pensée sauvage* (1962). Rpt. Paris: Plon, 1990, 279–280.
3. Craig Calhoun, Paul Price, and Ashley Timmer, eds., *Understanding September 11*. New York: New Press, 2002.
4. Jim Dwyer and Kevin Flynn, *102 Minutes: The Untold Story of the Fight to Survive Inside the Twin Towers*. New York: Times Books, 2005.
5. Guy Peellaert and Nik Cohn, *Rêves du 20e siècle*. Paris: Grasset, 1999.
6. American historians immediately devoted a special issue to the event: "History and September 11," *Journal of American History*, 89, no. 2 (2002). For the diversity of arguments about September 11, see Jean Baudrillard, *L'esprit du terrorisme*. Paris: Galilée, 2001; Noam Chomsky, *9-11*. New York: Seven Stories Press, 2001; Jean-Marie Colombani, *Tous Américains?: Le monde après le 11 septembre 2001*. Paris: Fayard, 2002; Alexandre Adler, *J'ai vu finir le monde ancien*. Paris: Grasset, 2002; Jacques Derrida and Jürgen Habermas, *Le concept du 11 septembre. Dialogues à New York (octobre-décembre 2001) avec Giovanna Borradori*. Paris: Galilée, 2004.
7. François Hartog, ed., *L'Histoire d'Homère à Augustin. Préface des historiens*. Paris: Seuil, 1999, 100: "By the posture that he adopts, the historian [Thucydides] intends to address his history to future readers,

transmitting to them, with this narrative to which he gave forever the name of *The Peloponnesian War*, a tool for understanding future present moments. Taking into account what men [*to anthrôpinon*] are, other analogous crises will not fail to occur in the future. For Thucydides, it is this permanence of human nature that grounds the exemplary nature of this conflict."

8. In the sense Georg Simmel gives to this term. See David Frisby, *Fragments of Modernity: Theories of Modernity in the Work of Simmel, Kracauer, and Benjamin*. Cambridge: Polity, 1985, 6. See also Sylviane Agaciniski, *Le passeur de temps. Modernité et nostalgie*. Paris: Seuil, 2000.
9. Sadik M Al-Azm, "Time Out of Joint. Western Dominance, Islamist terror, and the Arab Imagination." *Boston Review*, October-November 2004.
10. Noam Chomsky, "Terrorisme, l'arme des puissants." *Le Monde Diplomatique*, December, 2001, 10–11: "Mr. Ben Laden was the product of the United States' victory over the Soviets in Afghanistan; what will their new triumph in this country cost?"
11. Jean Baudrillard, *L'esprit du terrorisme*, op. cit.
12. Eric Darton, *Divided We Stand. A Biography of New York's World Trade Center*. New York: Basic Books, 1999.
13. Ibid., 119.
14. One of the novelists who has made abundant use of the theme of the double and twins is Michel Tournier (*Les Météores, Le Roi des Aulnes*, etc. Regarding this apsect of Tournier's work, see the second part of Arlette Bouloumié's book *Michel Tournier: le roman mythologique*. Paris: José Corti, 1988.
15. René Girard, *La Violence et le sacré*. Paris: Grasset, 1972, 59–88.
16. See Mary Douglas, *Purity and Danger : An Analysis of Concepts of Pollution and Taboo*. New York: Praeger, 1966.
17. *Le Monde*, September 29, 2001.
18. Françoise Héritier, *Masculin/Féminin. La pensée de la différence*. Paris: Odile Jacob, 1996; *Masculin/Féminin II: Dissoudre la hiérarchie*. Paris: Odile Jacob, 2002.
19. Nilüfer Göle, *Melez Desenler. Islam ve Modernlik Üzerine*. Istanbul: Metis Yayinlari, 2000.
20. For the "clash" thesis, see Samuel Huntington, *The Clash of Civilizations and the Remaking of World Order*. New York: Simon & Schuster, 1996.
21. Nilüfer Göle, "Ingénieurs islamistes et étudiantes voilées en Turquie." In Gilles Kepel and Yann Richard, eds., *Intellectuels et militants de l'islam contemporain*. Paris: Seuil, 1990.
22. Nilüfer Göle, *Musulmanes et modernes. Voile et civilisaiton en Turquie*. Paris: La Découverte, 1993; rpt. 2003.
23. A term used by Farhad Khosrokhavar, "Les nouveaux martyrs d'Allah." *Le Monde*, October 2, 2001. Cf. his book with the same title, *Les Nouveaux martyrs d'Allah*. Paris: Flammarion, 2003.

Chapter 4

1. For a history of terrorism, cf. Gérard Chaliand and Arnaud Blin, *Histoire du terrorisme de l'Antiquité à Al Qaïda*. Paris: Balland, 2004.
2. Cf. Gilles Kepel, *Jihad, expansion et déclin de Islamisme*. Paris: Gallimard, 2000.
3. *Le Monde*, December 1, 2003.
4. On the "witness" and the "martus," see François Hartog's article, "Le témoin et l'historien." *Gradhiva*, no. 27, July 2000, 1–14..
5. Cf. Farhad Khosrokhavar, *les Nouveaux martyrs d'Allah*, op. cit.
6. Ulrich Beck, "Cosmopolitical Realism: On the Distinction between Cosmopolitanism in Philosophy and in the Social Sciences." *Global Networks: A Journal of Transnational Affairs*, April, 2005, vol. 4, no. 2, 131–156. Cf. the same author's *Riskogesellschaft. Auf dem Weg in eine andere Moderne*. Frankfurt a. M.: Suhrkamp, 1986. *Risk Society: Towards a New Modernity*, trans. Mark Ritter. London and Thousand Oaks, CA: Sage, 1992.
7. Esther Benbass, *Une diaspora sépharade en transition (Istanbul, XIXe-XXe siècles)*. Paris: Cerf, 1993.
8. On Sayyid Qutb, see Gilles Kepel, *Le Prophère et le Pharaon. Aux sources des mouvements islmaistes*. New ed., Paris: Seuil, 1993; Olivier Carré, *Mystique et politique. Le Coran des islmaistes. Lecture du Coran par Sayyid Qutb, Frère musulman radical (1906–1966)*. Paris: Cerf, 2004; Paul Berman, *Les Habits neufs de la terreur*, op. cit. See also Roger Pol-Droit, "Le maître à penser de l'islamisme radical." *Le Point*, September 9, 2004, 92.
9. Jason Burke, *Al-Qaeda. Casting a Shadow of Terror*. New York and London: I.B. Tauris, 2003.
10. Katrin Bennhold, "Leaders of Turkey and Israel Clash at Davos Panel," *The NewYork Times,* January 29, 2009.
11. Thomas L. Friedman, "Letter from Istanbul," *The NewYork Times,* June 15, June 21, 2010.
12. Elliot Hen-Tov and Bernard Haykel, "Turkey's Gain Is Iran's Loss," *The NewYork Times,* June 21, 2010.
13. Bernard Guetta, "Encore un effort, M. Recep Erdogan," Liberation, September 6, 2010.

Chapter 5

1. Arjun Appadurai, *Après le colonialisme. Les conséquences culturelles de la globalisation*. Paris: Payot, 2005.
2. That is notably the case for the interpretation given priority by Thomas Friedman, *TheWorld Is Flat*. New York: Farrar Strauss Giroux, 2005.

3. Talal Asad raises this crucial question: cf. *Genealogies of Religion. Discipline and Reasons of Power in Christianity and Islam*. Baltimore and London. Johns Hopkins University Press, 1993, 7–12.
4. Francis Bacon represented the "advancement of learning" by a ship sailing beyond the pillars of Hercules into the open sea. On the interpretation of this frontispice, cf. François Hartog, *Anciens, Modernes, Sauvages*. Paris: Galaade, 2005.
5. Cf. Jürgen Habermas, *Strukturwandel der Öffentlichkeit*. Neuwied: Luchterhand, 1962. By the same author, "L'espace public, 30 ans après,." *Quaderni*, 18 (Autumn 1992), 161–191. On the concept of the public sphere, see Isabelle Paillart, ed., *L'Espace pubic et l'emprise de la communication*. Grenoble: Ellug, 1995. See also Chantal Mouffe, *Le Politique et ses enjeux. Pour une démocratie plurielle*. Paris: La Découverte/MAUSS, 1994.
6. Axel Honneth, *La Lutte pour la reconnaissance*. Paris: Cerf, 2000. Cf. Reinhart Koselleck, *Le Règne de la critique*. Trans. H. Hildenbrand. Paris: Minuit, 1979.
7. Cf. Olivier Roy, *L'Islam mondialisé*, op. cit., 153.
8. Dick Howard, "Quand l'Amérique rejoint tragiquement le monde." *Esprit*, October 2001, 8–14.
9. Richard Powers, "The Smile," *The New York Times*, September 23, 2001.
10. Olivier Roy, *L'Islam mondialisé*. Paris: Seuil, 2002.
11. Michel Wieviorka, "Terrorisme, une rupture historique." *Ramsès*, 2003, 29–42.
12. Let us recall the publication of Michel Houellebecq's book, apparently a case of fiction anticipating reality: *Plateforme* was published toward the end of August, 2001 (Paris: Flammarion).
13. Craig Calhoun, "The Emergency Imagination," a paper presented at a conference in honor of Charles Taylor, "Secularizations, Multiple Modernities, Social Imaginations," Northwestern University, July 10, 2002.
14. Alain Touraine, *Pouvons-nous vivre ensemble?Égaux et différents*. Paris: Balland, 2001, 62–69.
15. For a study of the case of the headscarf in the Turkish parliament, see Nilüfer Göle, "La deuxième phase de l'islamisme, l'expérience turque." In Michel Wieviorka and Jocelyne Ohana, eds., *La Différence culturelle. Une réformulaton des débats*. Paris: Balland, 2001, 62–69.
16. For an elaboration of this concept of a social imagination (*imaginaire social*), cf. *Public Culture*, 14, no. 1 (2002), "New Imaginaries."
17. Michael Wieviorka, "Réflexions sur le 11 septembre et ses suites." *Confluences* 40, Winter 2001–2002.
18. Cf. Charles Taylor, *Sources of the Self: The Making of the Modern Identity*. Cambridge MA: Harvard UP, 1989. Cf. Jerrold Siegel, *The Idea of the Self: Thought and Experience in Western Europe since the Seventeenth Century*. Cambridge: Cambridge UP, 2005.

Chapter 6

1. Abdelwahab Meddeb, *La Maladie de l'Islam*. Paris: Seuil, 2002.
2. On the notion of translation in the human sciences, cf. Hayden White, *The Content of the Form*. Baltimore: Johns Hopkins UP, 1987, 188–189.
3. Gilles Deleuze, "Les conditions de la question: qu'est-ce que la philosophie?" In *Prétentaine* 5, May 1996, "Philosophie et postmodernité," 19–25. Gilles Deleuze and Félix Guattari, *Qu'est-ce que la philosophie?* Paris: Minuit, 1991. Cf. Toni Negri's review in *Multitudes*, December 1991.
4. For philosophy as the force of the concept, cf. Jean-Marie Brohm, "Le concept comme style," op. cit. 10.
5. Talal Asad, *Genealogies of Religion*. London and Baltimore: Johns Hopkins UP, 1993.
6. Cf. Bill Ashcroft, Gareth Griffiths, and Telen Tiffin, eds., *The Empire Writes Back: Theory and Practice in Post-Colonial Literatures*. New York: Routledge, 2002. But see also Homi K. Bhaba, *The Location of Culture*. New York: Routledge, 1994.
7. Talal Asad, *Genealogies of Religion*, op. cit., 8–12.
8. Daniel Lerner, *The Passing of Traditional Society: Modernizing the Middle East*. London: Macmillan, 1958.
9. Cf. Nicole Lapierre, *Penser ailleurs*. Paris: Stock, 2005.
10. Schmuel Noah Eisenstadt, *Comparative Civilizations and Multiple Modernities*. Leyden and London: Brill, 2003.
11. Cf. Levent Yilmaz, "The Vanishing of the East." *Intellectual News*, no. 5–6, 2000. (A longer version of this article appeared in Turkish in *Baticilik Modernlik*, ed. Tanl Bora. Istanbul: Iletisim Yayinlari, 2002).
12. For an approach to cultural modernity in China that empahsizes this break with the past and "ruthless forgetting," see Ching-kiu Stephen Chan, "Beyond the Cultural Dominant: For a Textual Politics in Modern China." *Tsing Hua Journal of Chinese Studies*, 19, no. 2 (1989), 125–163.
13. Levent Yilmaz, "The Vanishing of the East," op. cit.; cf. *Le Temps moderne. Variations sur les Anciens et les contemporains*. Paris: Gallimard, 2004.
14. Ackbar Abbas, "Building on Disappearance: Hong Kong Architecture and the City." *Public Culture*, 6 (1994), 448–449.
15. Here we use the term *veil* in the generic sense, to designate the Muslim woman's obligation to cover her hair and conceal the shape of her body in order to respect Islamic values of feminine modesty; it includes both the Arab *hijab* and the Turkish *tessettür*. For an analysis of veiled women and their relation to modernity, cf. Nilüfer Göle, *Musulmanes et modernes. Voile et civilisation en Turquie*. op. cit.

Chapter 7

1. On this subject, see Milan Kundera's crucial remarks in his most recent novel, *Le Rideau* (Paris: Gallimard, 2005, 43–72). These same pages are quoted by Juan Goytisolo in "Kundera explore le roman," *Le Nouvel Observateur*, April 7, 2005, who continues his reflection as follows: "Contrary to what people think, this terrorism arises not only among minority languages, which are often also persecuted languages (Czech, Slovak, Slovene, Catalan, Galician), but also in a larger space such as that of the Castilian language; this is due to barrier raised by academia and the publishing world between the Spanish novel and the Latin-American novel, and, within the latter, among the Mexican, Argentine, Colombian, and Cuban novels, as if the boundaries between countries created artistic boundaries and marked out preserves. Literary works do not allow themselves to be imprisoned within the borders of their respective countries; on the contary, they inscribe themselves on the map of a geography unexplored by their predecessors. The professionals of nationalism and ineptitude (the two generally go together) accuse Flaubert (as did Montherlant and Maurice Bardèche, cited by Kundera) of 'not being cut from the same cloth as a Racine, a Saint-Simon, a Chateaubriand, or a Michelet" in other words, of not being 'French enough,' as others have accused Gombrowicz of not being 'Polish enough, or Kundera himself, of not being Czech enough.' Now so far as the art of the novel is concerned, there are no nationalities other than the Rabelaisian, the Cervantine, the Flaubertian, to mention only the most famous. National, provincial, or local glories that have not discovered unexplored artistic territories are doomed to the dreary immortality of statues and commemorative plaques: that is, to the nullity of redundancy and futility."
2. Talal Asad, *Genealogies of Religon*, op. cit.
3. Charles Taylor, *Varieties of Religion Today*. Cambridge MA: Harvard UP, 2002, 83. By the same author, see *Modern Social Imaginaries*. Durham NC: Duke UP, 2004.
4. See for example the position of Charles Perrault regarding the Chinese, in Levent Yilmaz, *Le Temps Moderne*, op. cit., chap. 36: "Perrault's whole argument is summed up in the proposition that the Chinese share the space of the Moderns, but not their time; they are the Ancients by ignorance, not by virtue of a past time. The Chinese Ancients are the ancient Chinese, the Ancients of the (French) Ancients are the Ancients—the Greeks and Romans—who lived in a past space and time. As for the Moderns, they don't have any Ancients! The break, in the latter case, is irremediable. There is a time peculiar to Moderns, dissociated form general time. So that, paradoxically, Perrault has trouble circumscribing the Moderns' past. Maybe they don't have a past, as if they were 'born from the earth.'"

5. Johannes Fabian, *Time and the Other, How Anthropology Makes Its Object*. New York: Columbia UP, 1983.
6. François Hartog, *Régimes d'historicité*. Paris: Seuil, 2003.
7. Cf., for example, the debate regarding the revolutionary calendar: Bronisalw Baczko, "Le calendrier républicain." In *Les lieux de mémoire*, vol. 1 (1984), ed. Pierre Nora. Paris: Gallimard, 1997, 67–106.
8. Ernest Gellner, *Muslim Society*. Cambridge: Cambridge UP, 1981.
9. Danièle Hervieu-Léger, *La Religion pour mémoire*. Paris: Cerf, 1993; cf., by the same author, the following works: *Les Identités religieuses en Europe* (ed., with G. Davie), Paris: La Découverte, 1996; *La Religion en miettes ou la qustion des sectes*, Paris: Calmann-Lévy, 2002; *Catholicisme français: La fin d'un monde*, Paris: Bayard, 2003.
10. Norbert Elias, *The Civilizing Process*. Trans. Edmund Jephcott. 2 vols. New York: Pantheon, 1978–1982.
11. Dipesh Chakrabarty, *Habitations of Modernity: Essays in the Wake of Subaltern Studies*. Chicago: University of Chicago Press, 2002. By the same author, see *Provincializing Europe: Postcolonial Thought and Historical Difference*. Princeton NJ: Princeton UP, 2000.
12. Cf. the special issue of *Daedalus*, "Multiple Modernities," Winter, 2000 (vol. 129).

Chapter 8

1. This process of legitimation has not been smooth and harmonious; the military coups of 1960, 1971, and 1980 repeatedly interrupted it and political parties were banned. But after each coup, the transition toward democracy resumed and the same parties were formed again under different names, with the same leaders and the same organization. The National Order Party was created in 1970 by defectors from the center-right Justice Party (*Adalet Partisi*). After it was banned in 1971, it was refounded in 1972 under the name National Salvation Party (*Milli Selamet Partisi*) and in 1974–1975 took part in two coalition governments. The 1980 military coup led to another dissolution of the political parties. The Islamist party resurfaced in 1983 under the name Welfare Party (*Refah Partisi*). During the municipal elections of March 27, 1994, it obtained 19.09 percent of the vote, and then 21.3 percent in general elections held on December 25, 1995. But lay public opinion and the military brought down the coalition government that had emerged from the elections, prohibiting once again the Islamist party. The latter tried to regain political ground under the name of Virtue Party (*Fazilet Partisi*) before a second prohibition that led it to change its name yet again: Felicity Party (*Saadet Partisi*). At this point there was a break with the party's "modernists": in 2001, Recep Tayyip Erdoğan and his friends left Necmettin Ergakan and the Felicity Party to create the AKP, the Justice and Development Party

(*Adalet ve Kalkinma Partisi*).
2. Cornelius Castoriadis, *L'Institution imaginaire de la société*. Paris: Seuil/Esprit, 1975.
3. M. Sükrü Hanioğlu, *The Young Turks in Opposition*. New York and Oxford: Oxford UP, 1995, 3–32 *passim*.
4. For a comparison of *laïcité* in the two countries, see "Laïcité/*laiklik*: Introduction" in *Laïcité(s) en France et en Turquie*, ed. Jean-Paul Burdy and Jean Marcou, *CEMOTI* (*Cahiers d'études sur la Méditerranée orientale et le monde turco-iranien*), no. 19, 1995. Cf. the excellent work by Marcel Gauchet, *La Religion dans la démocratie. Parcours de la laïcité*. Paris: Gallimard, 1998.
5. Françoise Gaspard and Frahad Khosrokhavar, *Le Foulard et la République*. Paris: La Découverte, 1995.
6. *Laïcité(s) en France et en Turquie*, op. cit., 13.
7. Nilüfer Göle, "Authoritarian Secularism and Islamist Politics: The Case of Turkey." In Augustus R. Norton, ed., *Civil Society in the Middle East*, vol. 2. Leyden, New York, and Cologne: Brill, 1996.
8. Ernest Gellner, *Muslim Society*, op. cit., 68.
9. The Democratic Party (*Demokrat Parti*, DP), which was in power in 1950, owed its popularity to the fact that it had put an end to these imposed religious practices, but for the same reason the republicans condemned it as counter-revolutionary.
10. See Jocelyne Dakhlia, *Islamicités*. Paris: PUF, 2005.
11. Jürgen Habermas, *The Structural Transformation of the Public Sphere*. Trans. Thomas Burger. Cambridge, MA: MIT, 1991; Mary P. Ryan, "Gender and Public Access: Women's Politics in Nineteenth-Century America." In Craig Calhoun, ed., *Habermas and the Public Sphere*. Cambridge MA: MIT, 1993, 277.
12. Nilüfer Göle, *Musulmanes et modernes*, op. cit.

Chapter 9

1. We find in Auguste Comte this kind of interpretation of human progress and enlightened reason connected with the phases of universal becoming, or again in Condorcet: see *Esquisse d'un tableau historique des progrès de l'esprit humain* (1794), ed. Alain Pons. Paris: Flammarion, 1998.
2. François Hartog, *Anciens, Modernes, Sauvages*, op. cit.
3. Cécile Dauphin and Arlette Farge, eds., *Séducton et sociétés: approches historiques*. Paris: Seuil, 2001. Edited by the same authors, *De la violence et des femmes*. Paris: Albin Michel, 1997. Arlette Farge has also co-edited with Natalie Zemon Davis *Histoire des femmes, XVIe-XVIIIe siècle*. Vol 3, ed. G. Duby and M. Perrot. Paris: Plon, 1991.
4. Norbert Elias, *The Civilizing Process*, op. cit.

5. Ibid.
6. Ibid.
7. For a brief history of politeness and its conflict with sincerity, see the essay collection *Politesse et sincérité*. Paris: Esprit, 1994.
8. Marcel Mauss, Les techniques du corps" (1934). Rpt. in *Sociologie et anthropologie*. Paris: PUF, 2001, 14.
9. Ibid., 368–369.
10. Ibid., 368.
11. In my book *Musulmanes et modernes*, op. cit., the reader will find a detailed discussion of the debate and a list of the works cited.
12. Salhaddin Assim, *Türk Kadinliğinin Tereddisi yahut Karilaşmak (Osmanli'da Kadinliğin Durumu)*. Istanbul: Arba Yayinlari, 1989 (first edition 1950).
13. Celal Nuri Ileri (1877–1938), *Kadinlarimiz*. Ankara: Kultur Bakanaliği Yayinlari, 1993.
14. Halil Hamit, *Islamiyette Feminizm yahut Alem-i Nisvanda Musava-i Tamme (Kadinlik Aleminde Tam Eşitlik)*. In T. Taşkiran, Cumhuriyet'in 50. Yilina Turk Kadin Haklari, Başbakanlik Kültur Müsteşarliği, Başakanlik Basimevi, 1973, 53.
15. Said Halim Pasha, *Buhranlarimiz*. Tercüman 1001 Eser, Istanbul, 1919, 136.
16. Mehmet Tahir, *Meşrutiyet Hanimlari*. In Bernard Caporal, *Kemalizmde ve Kemalizm Sonrasinda Türk Kadini*. Iş Bankasi Kütur Yay., Ankara, 1982, 87.
17. Derviş Vahdeti, in Tarik Zafer Tunaya, *Islamcilik Cereyani*. Istanbul, 1962, 86.
18. Mehmet Akif, in Tarik Zafer Tunaya, op. cit., 7–8.
19. Peyami Safa, *Türk Inkilabina Bakişlar*. Istanbul: Kanaat Kitabevi, 1938, 51–112.
20. Marcel Mauss, *Sociologie et anthropologie*, op. cit., 381.
21. Marcel Gauchet, *Le Déenchantement du monde*. Paris: Gallimard, 1984.
22. Irène Théry, *Les Dilemmes de l'individualisme. Monde sexué et moi sexuel*. Paris: Odile Jacob, 2005.
23. Cf. Azade Kian-Thiebaut, *Les Femmes iraniennes entre Islam, État et famille*. Paris: Maisonneuve et Larose, 2002.
24. Marjo Buitelaar, "Public Baths as Private Places." In Karin Ask and Marit Tjomsland, eds., *Women and Islamization. Contemporary Dimensions of Discourse and Gender Relations*. Oxford and New York: Berg, 1988, 103–123.
25. I thank Jeannette Jouili (a student writing a thesis at the EHESS) for having provided me with this detail from her interviews.
26. Cf. Leila Ahmed, *Women and Gender in Islam. Historical Roots of a Modern Debate*. New Haven and London: Yale UP, 1992, 120.

Chapter 10

1. Nilüfer Göle, *Musulmanes et modernes*, op. cit.
2. As we saw in the preceding chaptaer. Nilüfer Göle, "Islam in Public: New Visibilities and New Imaginations," *Public Culture* 14 (2002), 173–190.
3. Erving Goffman, *Stigmata: Notes on the Management of Spoiled Identity*. Engelwood Cliffs, NJ: Prentice-Hall, 1963.
4. Up to that point, Turkey had very deliberately followed the French model and Jacobinism; now it is France that, without admitting it—for it is never considered proper to take the Turks as a model—is producing something similar to what is found in Turkey, with the institutionalization of religion, its supervision by the state, and the radicalization of the debate over the headscarf. Nonetheless, we must not forget that in France the question of Islam is connected with those of immigration and social integration.
5. Craig Cahoun, ed., *Habermas and the Public Sphere*. Cambridge: MIT, 1993.
6. Cf. François Furet, preface to Alexis de Toqueville, *De la démocratie en Amérique*. Paris: Garnier-Flammarion, 1981.
7. Bruno Latour, "Pourquoi Marianne n'a plus de lait." *Le Monde*, September 27, 2003.

Chapter 11

1. Riva Kastoryano, ed, *Quelle identité pour l'Europe? Le multiculturalisme à l'épreuve*. Paris: Sciences Po, 2005. By the same author, *La France, l'Allemagne et leurs immigrés: négocier l'identité*. Paris: Armand Colin, 1996.
2. Composed of twenty advisors, the Stasi commission was headed by Bernard Stasi and assigned to draw up an inventory of secularism in France and to come up with ideas for a proposed law prohibiting religious signs, and notably the headscarf, in schools. It delivered its recommendations on December 11, 2003. Cf. Patrick Weil, *La République et sa diversité*. Paris: Seuil, 2005. Cf., by the same author, "Lever le voile." *Esprit*, January 2005, 45–53.
3. Emmanuel Terray, "L'hystérie politique." In Charlotte Nordmann, ed., *Le Foulard islamique en questions*. Paris: Editions Amsterdam, 2004, 103–117).
4. In the course of this debate, many people probably changed their minds, but as Emmanuel Terray points out (ibid., p. 117), all these changes were in the same direction, from rejecting the law to accepting it. Thus Terray does not see in it a proof of open discussion, as some have claimed, but on the contrary an indication of a contagious hysteria.
5. Along this line of thought, Sidi Mohammed Barkat has developed a very

interesting argument by defending the notion that the law connects the act of wearing the veil with the political experience of the French and in reality carries out a profound transformation of the factual situation by creating the conditions for a new way of apprehending this object, both by those who wear it and those who oppose it. According to him, the law constitutes the institutional framework for a possible subjective transformation of the parties involved and a possible renewal of the exegesis of the founding texts of Islam. Cf. Sidi Mohammed Barkat, "La loi contre le droit." In Charlotte Nordmann, ed., *Le Foulard islamique en questions*, op. cit. 28–35.
6. On the strategies for liberating "daughters of North African immigrants," see Nacira Guenif Souilamas, *Des beurettes*. Paris, Hachette, 2003.
7. This connection between secularism and women's rights is, moreover, obvious when we place ourselves in the historical context of the Muslim countries.
8. Erving Goffman, *Stigma*, op. cit.
9. On this subject, see Fariba Adelkhah, *Être moderne en Iran*. Paris: Karthala, 1998, and Azadeh Kian-Thiebaut, *Les Femmes iraniennes entre islam, État et famille*. Paris: Maisonneuve et Larose, 2002.
10. Quoted by Florence Vinas, "Entre oui et non: Simmel, philosophe de l'âme moderne." In Georg Simmel, *La Parure et autres essais*. Paris: La Maison des sciences de l'homme, 1998.

Chapter 12

1. Jürgen Habermas, *The Structural Transformation of the Public Sphere*, op. cit., 95.
2. Ibid., 98.
3. According to a poll published in *Le Figaro* for December 13, 2004, just before the European summit meeting on December 16–17, 67 percent of the French declared their opposition to Turkey's joining Europe; 39 percent because "human rights are not always respected there," and 34 percent because the "religious and cultural differences" were too great.
4. Pierre Rosanvallon, *Le Peuple introuvable. Histoire de la représentation démocratique en France*. Paris: Gallimard, 1998, 341–343.
5. Ibid., 344.
6. Ibid., 345.
7. Ibid.
8. Jürgen Habermas, *The Structural Transformation*, op. cit., 245.
9. One of the arguments thus consists in claiming that Europe's adversaries, England or the United States, are supporting Turkey's inclusion with the sole objective of weakening the Union.
10. For the development of this argument, cf. Nilüfer Göle, "La Turquie: le

désir d'Europe qui dérange." In Cengiz Aktar, ed., *Lettres aux turco-sceptiques*. Arles: Actes Sud, 2004.
11. Reinhart Koselleck, *L'Expérience de l'histoire*. Paris: Gallimard/Le Seuil, 1997, 188.

Chapter 13

1. Norbert Elias, *The Civilizing Process*, op. cit.

About the Author and Translator

Nilüfer Göle is a prominent Turkish sociologist and a leading authority on today's educated, urbanized, religious Muslim women. Göle has explored specifically the topic of covering, as well as the complexities of living in a multicultural world. Her sociological approach has also produced a broader critique of Eurocentrism with regard to emerging Islamic identities. Her seminars in various universities in Europe, Turkey, and the United States, her publications, and her public presentations have helped to create new horizons for social science research relating to the form of and issues surrounding the encounter between contemporary Islam and Europe. Moreover, her work informs other research fields, including migration studies, Islam, gender, anthropology, and political science.

Nilüfer Göle

A professor at Boğaziçi University in Istanbul from 1986 to 2001, Göle is currently director of studies at the École des Hautes Études en Sciences Sociales in Paris. She has been a visiting professor at MIT in Massachusetts and at the New School in New York.

Göle's first book, *Muslim and Modern*, which studied Islam through the prism of gender and modernity, has become a seminal work in sociology and gender studies and is now used as a standard reference for researchers working in different cultural contexts. She has highlighted in studies of contemporary Islam the centrality of women, piety, body, and the "private-public" distinction that fuels the conflict between the religious and the secular. In her research, she brings together students from many nationalities and from various academic institutions to promote mutual learning and intercultural exchange. *Islam in Public: Turkey, Iran, and Europe*, which Göle co-edited, is a comparative study on the emergence of Islam in various public spaces. *Islam in Europe* is her latest book (an expanded version of the French edition, *Interpénétrations: L'Islam et l'Europe,* and the German edition, *Anverwandlungen: Der Islam in Europa*), in which she argues that in the past two decades, Islam has become a decisive element of confrontation in the self-definition and self-presentation of Europeans. Many of Göle's books, including *The Forbidden Modern: Civilization and Veiling,* her pioneering work on the contemporary significance of the Islamic head scarf, have been translated into multiple languages.

Currently, Göle is conducting a European-scale research project entitled "Islam in the Making of a European Public Sphere," which is being funded by the European Research Council.

Steven Rendall is professor emeritus of Romance Languages at the University of Oregon and the author of numerous books and articles about French and European literature. He is also editor emeritus of *Comparative Literature*. He now lives in France and has translated over fifty books and fifty articles from French and German. Rendall has been the recipient of both the National Jewish Book Society's Sandra Brand and Arik Weintraub Award and the Modern Language Association's Scaglione Prize.

www.ingramcontent.com/pod-product-compliance
Lightning Source LLC
Chambersburg PA
CBHW020948230426
43666CB00005B/229